# THE
# TAX-SMART
## DONOR

Phil DeMuth

# THE
# TAX-SMART
## DONOR

OPTIMIZE
YOUR
LIFETIME
GIVING PLAN

Published by Alpha Dog Press, Los Angeles, California

This publication contains the author's opinions and is intended to provide accurate and authoritative information of a general nature. It is sold with the understanding that the author and publisher are not engaged in rendering specific legal, account-ing, investment planning, or other specific professional advice. Any accounting, legal, financial, business, or tax advice construed from its contents is not intended as a thorough, in-depth analysis of specific issues that can substitute for person-alized expert opinion. In all cases the reader should seek the services of qualified professionals for this. The author and publisher cannot be held accountable for any loss incurred as a result of specific investment or planning decisions made by the reader.

The tax-smart charitable dog on the cover is the work of renowned American cartoonist John Caldwell. Famous for his dogs, John was a proud member of *Mad* Magazine's Usual Gang of Idiots, then progressed to the *National Lampoon*, *The New Yorker*, *The Wall Street Journal*, and the *Harvard Business Review*, among many others. This dog was his last commissioned work.

ISBNs:
Hardcover: 978-0-9970596-4-9
eBook: 978-0-9970596-5-6

Printed in the United States of America
Book Design: 1106 Design
Cover Illustration by John Caldwell

Printed in the United States of America

# Table of
# **Contents**

# Introduction

In 2023, U.S. citizens gave roughly $557 billion to charity – far more than any other country. But who among us gave wisely, from a personal finance perspective?

- Do you have a large taxable estate (say, $50 million), and are you drawing up an estate plan near the end of your life? If so, you will work with sophisticated attorneys, investment advisors and accountants who will lay out the best charitable-giving strategies for your situation.
- Everyone else: not so much. . .

As an investment advisor, I notice that many highly intelligent people have little idea how to plan their charitable giving in the most tax-efficient, cost-effective manner. You can get good advice about how to deal with an ad hoc situation, but here's what you don't get: a lifetime charitable giving plan. Most charitable giving seems to be done haphazardly, often simply in response to being asked. This is a mistake. You will be a more powerful giver if you start with your own goals and build your plan from there. Optimizing your plan comes from giving in flow with the tax code instead of fighting it, and this means taking a lifetime perspective. By the time you finish this book, you will be able to sketch your optimal lifetime giving plan on the back of a napkin.

This was virgin territory, so I journeyed into the heart of the tax code.

What I learned:

- The tax code can either leverage your charitable giving or kneecap it. It is a powerful force for good or ill that needs to be considered and respected. There are a lot of rules to follow. You don't need to know them all, but you should know how to work with the ones that apply to you.

- Charitable giving should be managed holistically as an integral part of your financial planning. You do not want to become a charity case yourself. For most people, there is little intersection between their lifetime financial plans and their charitable giving, which seems to go out through a side channel when somebody puts their hand out. This is a missed planning opportunity.

- This requires becoming more intentional about your donations. You want to give when you can do the most good, when your dollars have the highest utility. Choose the best time to give. Take back the locus of control.

- While your money is an important component, even more important is the intelligence with which you deploy it. Study your charitable cause like a college course, preferably over years. This book has no opinion about which charities you should support. Some are better than others, but that part is up to you.
- Financial calculators can help you determine your most tax-efficient options: giving one way vs. another and giving now vs. later. These can help close the gap between your giving power and that of philanthropists who have attorneys and accountants on speed dial.

Here is a summary of what's coming in the chapters ahead. It offers a preview of the strategies that might be useful to you, as well as the ones you can pass over because they are irrelevant to your situation.

## Chapter One: How to Become a Tax-Efficient Giver

This chapter traces the history of the charitable deduction in U.S. tax law, introduced in 1917 to encourage philanthropic giving. It emphasizes the importance of leveraging the tax code to maximize charitable impact.

## Chapter Two: Types of Charities

Explains different charitable organizations and vehicles, including public charities, donor-advised funds, private foundations, and supporting organizations.

## Chapter Three: Tax Benefits

Covers various tax benefits related to charitable giving, including "above-the-line" and "below-the-line" deductions, and capital gains and estate tax avoidance.

## Chapter Four: Giving by Cash or Check

Discusses the simplicity but potential tax inefficiency of cash donations, especially considering the high threshold created by the standard deduction.

## Chapter Five: Donating Securities

Explores the tax advantages of donating appreciated securities, one of the most tax-efficient giving methods.

## Chapter Six: Retirement Account Philanthropy

Covers strategies like Qualified Charitable Distributions (QCDs) from IRAs and naming charities as beneficiaries of retirement accounts.

## Chapter Seven: Charitable Trusts

Primarily of interest to high-net-worth families, this chapter examines complex vehicles like Charitable Lead Trusts and Charitable Remainder Trusts.

## Chapter Eight: Prepackaged Gifts to Charity

Discusses options like charitable gift annuities and pooled income funds that offer scaled-down benefits with less upfront expense than custom trusts.

## Chapter Nine: Gifts of Property

Provides an overview of some of the complexities that accompany donating tangible property like art or real estate.

## Chapter Ten: Investing for Charity

Offers guidance on how to invest charitable dollars for maximum returns as well as when facing typical constraints.

## Chapter Eleven: Three Scenarios for Tax Strategy

Introduces the concept of "Giving Power" to evaluate the tax efficiency of various approaches while providing practical examples of how the strategies discussed in this book can be used.

## Chapter Twelve: Life-Cycle Charitable Giving

Outlines a paradigm for optimizing charitable giving across different life stages, considering factors like increasing donor knowledge, asset compounding, and changing tax patterns over the life cycle.

As we go to press, the Republicans have taken over Congress and the Presidency. They are likely to extend the Tax Cuts and Jobs Act past 2025. If they change the law in ways that will affect charitable planning as outlined in this book, I will address it in my website, www.phildemuth.com. The calculators available there should hold through 2025.

Chapter One

# Becoming a Tax-Efficient Giver

*"The meaning of life is to find your gift. The purpose of life is to give it away."*

- PABLO PICASSO

The charitable deduction is one of the oldest tax deductions. Our income tax dates to 1913, and the charitable deduction to 1917. This deduction was not some boondoggle for the rich. Gilded Age barons like Rockefeller and Carnegie were donating their fortunes to charity before the income tax came along.

Here's what happened:

When the income tax was introduced, the highest tax rate was a mere 15%. However, four years later, it had skyrocketed to 67%. The rationale for the tax hike was Woodrow Wilson's calamitous decision to plunge the U.S. into World War I. This illustrates how seemingly small taxes can quickly balloon into enormous proportions once politicians realize they have a new supply of funds to fuel their projects.

Congress was rightfully worried that a 67% tax rate would discourage wealthy individuals from giving to charity. After all, with the government taking such a big slice of the pie, why not let it carry the load? But this raised an awkward question: who would pay for the universities, libraries, hospitals, concert halls, theaters, museums, and medical facilities that were vital to America's greatness? The strain on public funds would be enormous and everlasting. In the end, Congress wisely chose to leave these responsibilities to the wealthy. The tax exemption for charitable donations passed with no opposition.

Charities naturally are aware that rich people would rather give their money to them than truck it to Washington, D.C. At least the charities host parties and list their donors as "philan-thropists." By comparison, the IRS offers no galas and provides little in the way of taxpayer appreciation.

Most donors do not want to pay taxes on the money they send to charity. You can be a far more effective giver when you donate directly to your charity of choice and skip the side payoff to the tax man along the way. You may not even be aware you are doing this since the donation and the tax can occur many months apart. What you really want is to enlist the government to underwrite your charitable giving instead of taxing it.

When your life is over, and the accountant in the sky adds up where you spent all the money that passed through your hands, who will be recipient number one, and by a wide margin? Answer: the U.S. Treasury. The government is your silent partner in all your financial transactions. But Uncle Sam has a borderline personality where your charitable giving is concerned. There are certain times when he wants to donate right alongside you, and other times when he will kick you in the teeth. The good news is that we can predict his mood in advance.

We may sometimes speak of using your dollars to "buy" charity (i.e., charitable goods and services). It sounds odd when put this way, but it is accurate. We will compare different ways of giving and score them according to how much it costs to buy a dollar's worth of charity after-tax. You can buy more charity when you only pay 60 cents on the dollar than when you spend 100 cents – or even 150 cents – on the dollar. If we had an infinite amount of money, it would not matter. Since our resources are finite, we want to do as much good as we can with what we have. This is basic stewardship.

You will be a more potent giver when you leverage your giving, and the easiest way to do this is to use the power of compounding: compounding your knowledge about the social ills you want to rectify, compounding your savings, and then using the tax code's charitable deductions to lever the good you do. This insight turns out to be sufficiently powerful that it can be worth reverse engineering your lifetime giving strategy in its light.

This roundup will look at vehicles for charitable giving, from the cash in your wallet to complicated trusts. It will look at different amounts of gifting*, from spare change to millions of dollars. We will explore the tax benefits that might be available.

The tax code is not a Platonic form of Truth and Beauty, but four million words of rules and regulations piled on top of more rules and regulations, with a dollop of fifteen thousand pages of tax law interpretation on the top. How did our government ever come to show such contempt for its citizens? Americans spend $2 billion annually attempting to comply with these

---

* Interrupting my Bohemian Grove breakfast with William F. Buckley Jr. someone at a nearby table spoke loudly of "gifting" something. Bill turned to him and said, "I'm sorry, you can't be my friend if you are going to use 'gift' as a verb." I will endeavor to follow Buckley's sensible practice in this book.

esoteric provisions. The tax code gives people what philosopher Ludwig Wittgenstein called a "mental cramp." If you feel dazed and confused, this often shows that you have understood the material correctly.

The goal of this book is to teach you how to be a more powerful giver by working in harmony with the tax code, which is not as easy as it sounds. Tax optimization comes from assiduously following the relevant rules. Do not assume that your intuition about what should work or might work or what makes sense is correct. Especially as the dollars get higher, run everything by qualified tax advisors.

We will consider how to buy charity, sliced and diced by topic. There will be some unavoidable overlap in these discussions but nothing too repetitious—especially when it comes to an approach that might work for you. Scan this book for ideas, read whatever applies to you, and skip the parts that do not. Don't tie your brain in knots trying to follow the intricacies of some complicated strategy you will never use. I will try to explain the points clearly, but in some cases, you will be experiencing the complexity of the tax code itself, which is not for the faint of heart. If this is for a strategy that is relevant to you, dig in. Otherwise, turn the page. If you don't, you will get bogged down in hopeless legal and accounting detail and you will hate reading it. If you stick to the parts that are about you, this book will be your friend. The goal is not for you to become an expert on the tax code, heaven forbid. The goal is for you to be able to give significantly more money to charity for the same out-of-pocket dollars.

There is a saying in finance, "Don't let the tax tail wag the dog." In other words, don't let minor details control important decisions. But in the case of charity, the dog and the tail have traded places, and tax considerations are paramount--we just never got the memo. The tax dog needs to wag the charity tail.

## Chapter Two

# Types of
# **Charities**

Like the warrior Arjuna in the *Bhagavad Gita*, we begin by surveying the battlefield before us. We'll start by reviewing the types of charitable organizations waiting to take our money.

## Registered Public Charities

These charities are registered under section 501(c)(3) of the Internal Revenue Service code, which is probably why they are referred to as "501(c)(3)" charities. They are the ones you can contribute to and claim a tax deduction. Every public charity you have heard of is a 501(c)(3) nonprofit. They call themselves "public charities" because they are supported by the public. However, private foundations are also 501(c)(3) tax-exempt organizations. They call themselves "private foundations."

What both have in common is that they operate for the public benefit, a concept nowhere defined. Often, their activities are religious, educational, scientific, medical, environmental, artistic, or involved in community service, mainly without government supervision.

In practice, a charity is a charity if it is listed on the IRS website under their "Tax Exempt Organization Search."

https://apps.irs.gov/app/eos/

If in doubt, look it up. Unfortunately, this tool is clunky. First, try searching by the charity's name. If that doesn't work, remember that the charity may have a legal name that is different from the name you know. For example, GiveWell (the Effective Altruism charity) is nowhere to be found because it turns out they are registered as The Clear Fund. I had to write GiveWell to get their Federal Tax ID (20-8625442) and look them up that way. This lack of a simple cross-referenced common name charity search is yet another government-created obstacle to charitable giving.

Once you land on the charity's page, you will see the charity's Deductibility Code (ideally "PC" for public charity) and the percentage-of-income limits that would apply to your gift (more on this later).

# Donor-Advised Funds

I immediately want to call your attention to Donor-Advised Funds (DAFs) since I will be referring to them endlessly. A DAF is a special type of 501(c)(3) public charity where each donor's contribution is tracked separately as a segregated account. Fidelity Investments created its DAF in 1991, and Schwab and Vanguard followed soon after. Today, these are some of the largest charities in the world. They have become indispensable for many people's charitable tax planning. You might say donor-advised funds are charitable IRAs.

For most people, donating appreciated stock to charity is the most tax-effective way to give, yet many small charities are not set up to process this kind of contribution. Donor-advised funds are experts in turning appreciated stock into cash that any charity will be able to digest easily.

DAFs function as a waystation for your charity dollars. In this holding tank, you can park and invest money indefinitely before passing it through to the ultimate destination charities you select. The DAF allows you, the donor, to recommend the amount for it to send to the 501(c)(3) public charity you nominate. In the meantime, the DAF takes over all the administrative, reporting, and investment responsibilities. Legally, once you donate money to them, they are entitled to invest and dispense it however they want. Your recommendation is nonbinding. But in practice, they will follow your wishes because if they stopped taking instructions from donors, that would be the end of them. You have de facto control but not legal control. That is the donor's implicit compact with the DAF.

DAFs have become especially popular since the Trump Tax Cuts and Jobs Act of 2017 (which is our current tax code). Today, there are about a thousand DAF sponsors sprinkled around the country, but I will focus on three: Fidelity, Schwab, and Vanguard. These are conveniently located at the brokerage houses where America's middle class and high net worth invest their money. You can set up a DAF account online with any of them in about fifteen minutes.

Fidelity, Schwab, and Vanguard let you choose from a menu of investment options that include low-cost market index funds. Then, to "recommend" a charitable distribution, you select the destination from a pull-down menu of all public and verified 501(c)(3) charities. You control the degree of anonymity or recognition desired when making a distribution. Even if the check is sent from "the Jones Family fund," the end charity cannot look up the amount of money behind it. The Jones Family Fund might own a bus token, a stick of gum, and some pocket lint, or it might hold $500 million. That said, never underestimate a charity's ability to size up your net worth. They may know more about your net worth than you do. If you prefer not to be hassled by more solicitations, make the gift anonymously.

The Big Three DAFs provide a lot of convenience and flexibility, and Fidelity and Schwab have a low minimum initial investment threshold that makes them easy to engage. The donor receives a charitable deduction for the donation when it is first given to the DAF, even though they might not elect to distribute the proceeds to the end charities until years later. The donor controls the timing for the initial donation and its ultimate disbursement. This can be very useful for personal tax planning in the first case and charitable planning in the second.

The convenience does not end there. Say you make a number of charitable donations every year—$500 here, $100 there, $300 someplace else, and so on. You no longer need to track these like a bloodhound to make sure every charity sends you an acknowledgment to keep in a shoebox for your accountant. Your only charity is the DAF. They will send you the documentation you need, and if you lose it you can easily go online and download it again.

*Rules:* There is no second charitable deduction available from the final pass-through donations, even if the end charity mistakenly sends you a tax acknowledgment letter. The donor can receive no benefit directly or indirectly from the final gift, and the DAF will be extremely picky on this point because the IRS is. These benefits might include invitations to charity galas, tickets, or the payment of any portion of a membership fee. Those will be entirely out-of-pocket from you.

Here is an idea that you are not the first to think of: What if you send $100,000 from your DAF to Princeton, with the tacit understanding that Princeton will designate a matching scholarship for your daughter next year? Answer: no, you cannot do that. One person went to jail for five months for tax evasion because he used a DAF to pay private school tuition.

For most people, the optimal way to fund a DAF is by donating appreciated stock containing significant embedded capital gains. The DAF can receive stock from anywhere, but this process works seamlessly if you already have your investment accounts at the same custodian ( i.e., Fidelity Brokerage Account to a Fidelity DAF). The DAF then grabs the exact shares of the securities you specify from your investment account, sells them, and invests the proceeds into the DAF mutual fund you designate. This may not sound like much but try getting your brokerage account to send the shares to some other institution, and you will appreciate this click-through service.

The ability to parcel out gifts over time is highly desirable. You can make one large tax-effective donation to the DAF to begin and then parcel it out in smaller donations that otherwise would not be tax-effective if they were spread out over the years. There is currently no 5% annual distribution requirement for DAF donors the way there is for private foundations. This delay option lets you be more prudent and thoughtful in your giving. Your ideas might change over time. You may be disappointed with a charity you previously supported or discover a new charity you like better. There's no long-term commitment. There are always cries (usually from people who don't give to charity) to force DAFs to expel their funds via required minimum distributions, but this is a complete nonissue. Fidelity, Schwab, and Vanguard donors give away close to 20% of their endowments annually.

Charitable giving can depend on the state of the economy. Here, a DAF can act as a useful buffer. You can donate to the DAF during bull markets and parcel out the donations to your end charities during lean years when they might have a harder time attracting contributions.

Charities, naturally, are interested in what you are going to do for them in the future. If you donate everything up front, you might discover that later that they don't greet you with the same enthusiasm as if your gift were still eagerly anticipated. Giving over time is one way to keep them engaged if that is of interest. Charities are happy to build long-term relationships.

## DAF Expenses

Fidelity and Schwab's DAFs charge $100 minimum or 0.60% of your account balance annually on accounts up to $500,000, with lower fee tiers on larger amounts. You can invest your donation in a U.S. Total Stock Market Index fund very cheaply. The actively managed mutual funds promoted on their menus charge much more, so be careful. If your financial advisor custodies accounts at Fidelity or Schwab, they can open and manage your DAF, although this will add another layer of fees. Money grows tax-free inside the DAF.

| TABLE 2.1: EXPENSES AT THE BIG 3 DONOR-ADVISED FUNDS | | | |
|---|---|---|---|
| | Vanguard | Fidelity | Schwab |
| Minimum $ to Open | $25,000 | $0 | $0 |
| Minimum $ to Add | $5,000 | $0 | $0 |
| Minimum $ Grant | $500 | $50 | $50 |
| Administrative fee (up to $500,000) | 0.60% | 0.60% | 0.60% |
| Fee on last dollar of $5,000,000 | 0.12% | 0.15% | 0.15% |
| U.S. Stock Market Index Fund Annual Fee | 0.02% | 0.02% | 0.03% |

These funds, having economies of scale, can get you set up and invested for no more than 0.63% a year. This compares favorably with the average DAF fee of 0.87% a year. Despite the fees, these DAFs subsidize their smaller accounts (say, under $100,000). The fees go toward the cost of tax reporting, the online platform, customer service, due diligence, and the fulfillment of grant requests. The less transparency you find about administrative fees and investment expenses on another DAF's website, the higher these are likely to be relative to Vanguard, Fidelity, and Schwab.

There is a sweet spot for using DAFs in midlife. Most people in their twenties don't have highly appreciated stock, and their tax rates are generally low. DAF fees can add up when compounded on small balances over decades. But middle-aged people may find themselves better positioned to use a vehicle like this during their high-income years after their stocks have had a chance to grow for a few decades. This is the best charity deal most people will see until they turn 73 and start pulling Required Minimum Distributions from their Individual Retirement Accounts. At that point, using Qualified Charitable Distributions becomes a lively option, as we will discuss later.

DAFs are also good vehicles for estate planning for well-off families. They might want to leave a traditional IRA to a family

DAF where 100% of its value will go to charity for the next generation's charitable giving. This might be either alongside or in preference to leaving the money to a private family foundation.

Another use case: imagine that your family started a hot dog stand forty years ago that has grown into a regional chain worth $20 million. You plan to sell the business but hate the thought of paying all the capital gains taxes. You could work with a DAF as you negotiate the sale. They might accept a share of the business, receive cash (untaxed) for the stock you gave them at the close, and leave your family a large charitable account to distribute over decades. You, in turn, would keep a share of the business and pay capital gains taxes on just the piece you retained while picking up an offsetting tax deduction from the portion that went into the DAF. We will discuss these ideas in more detail later.

## Other types of DAFs

While Fidelity, Schwab, and Vanguard are the biggest, thousands of regional DAFs are attached to various community foundations, charities, and religious groups. The DAFs linked to community foundations are especially worth calling out because many donors like to give locally. These community DAFs should have expertise on the charities in their geographic areas and so are a valuable source of boots-on-the-ground reconnaissance.

Gaining access to this knowledge base could easily justify their slightly higher fees.

One trend in philanthropy is for conservative charities to be run by liberal administrators once their founder/donors pass away (Ford Foundation, Pew Foundation, Rockefeller Foundation, etc.). As a result, there are now "theme" DAFs like the Bradley Impact Fund or Donor's Trust that limit distributions to a fixed menu of vetted conservative causes. Using one of these would prevent your grandchildren from giving your money to whatever flavor-of-the-month crusades across campus next semester.

There can be DAFs affiliated with churches and universities. These DAFs typically require that a significant percentage of the assets be dedicated to the charitable causes they sponsor.

There are donor-advised funds that specialize in foreign charities. The need is often greater abroad, and the U.S. dollar goes further in developing countries than it does in Manhattan. CAF America, National Philanthropic Trust, Silicon Valley Community Foundation, Goldman Sachs Philanthropy Fund, as well as Fidelity and Vanguard, all have expertise here. They have processes for assessing "equivalency to U.S. charities" and "expenditure responsibility," which are technical require-ments. They also have experience with international regulations and compliance issues, as well as resources for conducting due diligence on foreign charities. If you have a particular foreign charity in mind and cannot find a "backdoor" charity in the U.S. that funnels support directly to them, these DAFs would be a good place to start. Otherwise, giving money to foreign charities can be problematic. You might have to donate through a private foundation or through your will.

## Benefits of using a donor-advised fund:

- DAFs are the private foundations of America's middle class
- Availability of anonymous donations; not getting spammed with nuisance requests from charities and their call centers and junk mailing lists
- Ease of contributing shares of stock or mutual funds from your same-custodian accounts
- One-click donations save you time and trouble
- Let you use stock to give to charities unable to process noncash donations
- Possibility of tax savings by compressing multiple years' donations into a single year
- Tax-free compounding to help offset DAF management fees vs. the tax drag of holding securities in taxable accounts
- Availability of super-low-fee, market-wide index funds (if you hunt for them)

- No worries about tracking down multiple letters of acknowledgment and crossing your fingers that they are actually IRS-compliant
- Ability to feed multiple charities over multiple years from a single donation
- Ease of making recurring gifts to the same charity: set it and forget it
- Ease of separating your (aggressive) charity investment strategy from your (balanced or conservative) personal investment strategy
- Fidelity and Schwab accept Bitcoin, as will Vanguard on a case-by-case basis
- Effectively creating a generational family giving tool

## Private Foundations

A private foundation is a 501(c)(3) charitable legal corporation funded by an individual, a family, or a corporation. It usually is governed by a private individual or a board of directors chosen by the donor, such as family members. This foundation may exist in perpetuity and has a wide range of latitude and discretion over what it can do. I would suggest a million dollars as a minimum to open one.

The establishing documents specify the foundation's charitable intent, which can be for religious, scientific, literary, educational, or other charitable purposes. It cannot be used for political campaigns or lobbying. The board members and donors are forbidden from exploiting the charity for their own benefit.

The foundation files Form 1023 with the IRS to become a 501(c)(3) tax-exempt organization. After that, it files Form 990-PF annually, a public document that lists the foundation's revenues and expenses, executive compensation, capital gains and losses, and a summary of its charitable donations. It can be made more private by listing most of the information in Exhibits to Form 990-PF, which the IRS does not disclose except by special request. Fulfilling special requests can take time, especially from a government agency where it can take hours to get a human being on the phone.

A Private Foundation can be organized as a not-for-profit trust. This has certain advantages over organization as a not-for-profit corporation:

- Usually, no need to register with the Secretary of State
- Usually, no annual reports, fees, or filings at the state level
- Usually, no supervision at the state level
- All federal requirements still apply

A private foundation can make direct grants to public charities or sponsor their own charitable activities (including aid to specific individuals). They can make international grants. They can award scholarships and choose the recipients (but not to family members). They can fund public charities (including a donor-advised fund). In exchange for the higher startup costs and the administrative costs of annual reporting and tax filings, a private foundation offers more flexibility and control than a donor-advised fund.

Foundations pay an excise tax of 1.39% annually on their net investment income (interest, dividends, and capital gains), and they must spend down at least 5% of their endowment every year, based on the 12-month average of the endowment over the preceding tax year.

This minimum 5% annual payout encompasses gifts to charity as well as all customary and reasonable expenses of running the foundation. These might cover renting an office or buying an office building (the Gates Foundation has quite a nice one). It includes furniture, computers, software, utilities, office supplies, etc. It also covers salaries and benefits, trustee fees, consulting fees, travel expenses, research, publications, subscriptions, and so on. It encompasses legal and accounting expenses, such as preparing filings and tax returns and even publishing an annual report. The only requirement is that the money be spent responsibly. Any payout the foundation makes over 5% of its endowment in one year can be carried forward to meet this requirement over the next five years.

Although the 5% payout does not cover investment expenses (advisor fees, commissions, or board fees for investment oversight), these expenses do apply against the total to which the annual 1.39% excise tax applies. In the worst case, the private foundation could make a 5% gift to the family donor-advised fund to meet the annual requirement.

There are limits to the amount we can deduct from our taxes for our donations to charity. It depends on our income (technically, our *adjusted gross income* or AGI, a tax concept discussed later). The income-based donation limits to a private foundation are less generous than for a donor-advised fund or other public charities. Donors can contribute cash up to 30% and stock up to 20% of their adjusted gross income. Stock donated from your private company is limited to 10% of the company's value, *taken at its cost basis*. If you exceed these thresholds, you can stretch the deductions over five years (provided you have enough ongoing adjusted gross income to qualify). There are special rules for funding a foundation with real estate or other tangible personal property.

Private foundations are not supposed to be vehicles for wealthy families to grow their investment portfolios against a tax rate of 1.39% a year. Yet, with so much freedom and little oversight, there is room for abuse, self-dealing, related-party non-arm's-length transactions, undue influence from "disqualified" persons, etc., just as there is a corresponding freedom to do good. While the IRS nominally oversees these foundations, in practice the job often falls to the state attorney general's office. Your state attorney general typically has little in the way of time or resources to devote to this except in highly publicized cases.

A company called Foundation Source offers an easy way to open a turnkey foundation online at a reasonable expense (perhaps 1% or so). They keep their clients coloring within the lines and following all the rules. As with the major DAFs, their policies and procedures are designed to prevent rogue operators from getting them in trouble.

A private foundation can offer significant benefits to the founding family. The number one issue in these families is how to preserve the family values that made them successful (years of self-discipline, delayed gratification, grit, scrappiness, street smarts, economizing everywhere, relentless hard work) through the coming generations who have been given everything and acclimated themselves to soft living, with predictable bad results. A family foundation can work as a set of training wheels ostensibly to teach the next generation about charity, but in practice serving as a school that teaches the handling and investing of money as well as deploying it in sensible ways. It lets the founders test drive their succession planning while preparing the next generation for the responsibilities of wealth. To get started, grandparents might tell their children they can each donate $10,000 to any charity they wish this year and tell the grandkids they can similarly donate $1,000 apiece. This will elevate the family discussion around the Thanksgiving table. Later, annual board meetings can assemble relatives for a de facto seminar in finance and philanthropy. The family foundation provides a structure to glue the family together after the founders have left the building.

In olden days, superfluous sons not in line to inherit the family barony or run the family business could be packed off to the ministry or the army. Unwed daughters could go to a nunnery. These options are no longer popular. Today, employment at a private family foundation could offer a role for an adult child. There are trust-fund babies who wandered through their playing cards until one day the family foundation instilled a sense of mission to a world bigger than just themselves. My impression is that a full-time, qualified CEO of a small family foundation (say, $5 million in assets) might reasonably draw a salary of $150,000 plus benefits.

Table 2.2 compares Donor-Advised Funds to Private Foundations:

| TABLE 2.2: Donor-Advised Funds vs. Private Foundations | | |
|---|---|---|
| | Donor-Advised Funds | Private Foundations |
| **Max Deductions:** | | |
| **Cash** | 60% of AGI | 30% of AGI |
| **LT Gains** | 30% fair market value | 20% publicly traded stock |
| **Property** | 30% fair market value | 20% using cost basis |
| **Ann. Payout** | None | 5% |
| **Taxes** | None | 1.39% excise tax |
| **Startup Costs** | None | $5,000 on up |
| **Annual Costs** | 0.6% + fund expenses | 1% - 3% |
| **Privacy** | Yes | No |
| **# of them** | 1,286,000 | 130,000 |
| **Total Assets** | $234 billion | $1.3 trillion |
| **Grants in 2021** | $45 billion | $96 billion |

While the overwhelming number of private foundations engage solely in passive grantmaking, there are also Private Operating Foundations that actively run their charity projects. They are sort of midway between a Private Foundation and a Public Charity, and they have their own set of rules. Talk to your attorney about these if you want to run your own charitable programs.

Most people will be investing in 503(c)(3) public charities, but for the sake of completeness I should also mention:

# Limited Liability Companies (LLCs)

These have come into vogue for charity ever since Mark Zuckerberg and his wife, Priscilla Chan, opened the Chan Zuckerberg LLC. Their intention was to fund it with 99% of their Facebook (now Meta) stock, a mere $45 billion at the time.

The LLC is not a charity; any transactions would be reported on the Zuckerberg's' personal tax forms. It receives no tax benefits – those would only flow to the owners when the money it holds is dispensed to charity.

Since the LLC is not a charity, it does not have to follow any rules like giving away 5% of its portfolio every year. Its internal affairs can be kept private. There is no need to file a Form 990-PF as a private foundation would. Unlike a private foundation or a public charity, it is free to engage in political advocacy.

It can also invest in for-profit companies. The owners do not surrender their voting rights on any shares of securities the LLC holds, as they would if the shares were donated to a private foundation—an important consideration in the Zuckerberg's' case since it will be funded with large holdings of Meta stock. The LLC structure provides more freedom, control, and flexibility—but no up-front tax benefits and any investment income would continue to be taxed on the owner's returns every year. In theory, it could provide privacy—especially if their names were not on the title. They could keep their money in a coffee can and accomplish substantially the same goals (although it would have to be a large coffee can).

## Supporting Organizations

Sometimes, charities have *supporting organizations* to further their work.

If a charity's board members are not involved in fundraising, supporting organizations can be set up expressly to raise money.

Example: The Gates Foundation is a 501(c)(3) charitable foundation, but it does not need to raise money because it already has over $50 billion. It does not encourage donations but instead recommends that fans donate directly to the end charities they support (listed online in their grants database). However, the

Foundation recognizes that some people want to invest directly alongside them, so they have set up a supporting organization called Gates Philanthropy Partners, a 501(c)(3) public charity. Instead of trying to cook up great charity ideas on your own, it is perfectly reasonable to concede that Bill—no dummy—has a head start on you in this department and that your charitable dollars might be better spent under his organization's steward-ship than yours. This is the conclusion Warren Buffett came to.

## NONPROFITS THAT DO NOT OFFER A TAX DEDUCTION

Another category of nonprofits is designated as 501(c)(4) organizations. These promote social welfare (as they see it) and would love your financial support but can offer no tax benefit in return. Planned Parenthood would be one example, and the National Rifle Association another. They cannot involve them-selves in political campaigns, such as endorsing or opposing a candidate. However, with notice to members, they can and do lobby for or against specific pieces of legislation.

Additionally, both Planned Parenthood and the National Rifle Association have related 501(c)(3) public charities that limit themselves to purely charitable aspects of their work: the Planned Parenthood Federation of America and the NRA

Foundation. I highlight these as illustrative cases. Your favorite 501(c)(4) political organization might have a related 501(c)(3) charity you could support on a tax-deductible basis.

You cannot get a tax deduction for donating to overtly political organizations, such as the Democratic or Republican Parties, political action committees, or specific political campaigns or candidates.

However, determined givers have come up with workarounds. There are places where you can donate and receive a tax break where the organization is aligned with your political beliefs. For example, if you are a conservative, you might donate to the American Enterprise Institute, the Federalist Society, or Hillsdale College. Liberals might prefer the Brookings Institute, the Economic Policy Institute, or any other college.

The just-mentioned Zuckerbergs donated millions of tax-deductible dollars to support their favorite candidates in the 2020 election. With so much at stake, finding ways to donate tax-deductible dollars to support political candidates or specific pieces of legislation has become something of a black art. More recently, the Zuckerbergs seem to have grown disillusioned with investing in politics and sidelined their bets in 2024.

# Chapter Three

# Tax **Benefits**

*"All or a portion of philanthropic contributions can generate significant tax deductions for the donor. That benefit, however, is far from automatic."*

- WARREN BUFFETT

Here are the major types of tax benefits we will reference in the coming chapters. Some are more valuable than others. They don't fall into your lap. To get them, you need to claim them.

## "Above the line" deductions

Your Adjusted Gross Income (AGI) is a key figure in your tax return. It is calculated on page 1, line 11 of your federal income tax Form 1040. AGI includes all your annual income minus certain "above-the-line" deductions.

What are these "above-the-line" deductions? You'll find them on lines 1-10 of your tax form, right above where you report your AGI. That is what makes them "above the line," meaning above line 11. Some common examples include:

- Retirement plan contributions
- Health Savings Account (HSA) contributions
- Student loan interest payments

The great thing about above-the-line deductions is that they directly reduce your taxable income, dollar-for-dollar. A lower AGI means you pay less taxes overall. It can also help you qualify for other valuable credits and deductions. For example, the lower your AGI, the lower your potential capital gains taxes, dividend taxes, Medicare premiums, and tax on Social Security may be. So, the more you can claim in above-the-line deductions, the better.

The catch? Above-the-line deductions are rare. The IRS doesn't offer many of them. Qualified Charitable Distributions (QCDs) from your IRA accounts work the same way and with the same benefits, except they are not reported as income at all. We will dive into the details of QCDs later.

# "Below the line" tax deductions

These are miscellaneous items listed on Schedule A of your tax form, which appears a couple of pages after line 11 (and so they are called "below the line"). The most common deductions are for state and local taxes and home mortgage interest. Most charitable contributions get itemized on Schedule A as well. When people talk of "itemized" deductions, they are referring to Schedule A.

Here is the problem as far as taxes and charitable giving are concerned: Schedule A tax deductions are only claimed by about 10% of people who pay taxes. Everyone else uses the *standard deduction*, which is available to anyone without having to itemize anything.

The 2017 Tax Cuts and Jobs Act simplified tax filing by giving everyone a large standard deduction so people wouldn't have to bother with Schedule A. Adjusted every year for inflation, the standard deduction in 2025 is $15,000 for singles and $30,000 for those married filing jointly. Very few people are left in a position to itemize because most do not have enough itemized deductions to top the standard deduction. While tax simplification is an important goal, *one consequence of the large standard deduction is that many Americans no longer receive any tax benefit for giving to charity.*

If you and your spouse gave $30,000 to charity in 2025 and have no other deductions to report, you would receive no federal tax benefit from your gift because this amount is no more than the $30,000 standard deduction you could claim if you gave nothing. The standard deduction is the gaping chasm that must be filled before you can receive a tax benefit for charitable contributions.

The large standard deduction is a significant hurdle. Sadly, most small checks people write to charity will never add up to a number large enough to confer a tax benefit. That is one motivation for this book: to help you plan your charitable giving with the tax code in mind so you can get credit for as much of it as possible.

There are two widely claimed Schedule A deductions: one for State and Local Taxes or "SALT" (including property tax) and one for mortgage interest. These were both capped by the 2017 Tax Cuts and Jobs Act. The SALT tax deduction was capped at $10,000, and the mortgage interest deduction was capped at the acquisition interest on up to $1 million (or $750,000, depending on when the property was purchased). On average, this amounts to an $11,000 deduction for those who itemize, making the average combined claim for both SALT and mortgage interest around $21,000. A typical couple in this position would have to give $9,000 to charity to match the standard deduction before they could claim a dollar of credit for their charitable giving in 2025.

It gets worse.

The limits on the deductions for state and local taxes and mortgage interest were not adjusted for inflation. Because of the high inflation the country has undergone recently, the real value of a $10,000 deduction is now closer to $8,000 in today's dollars.

Meanwhile, the standard deduction was adjusted for inflation. As the value of the deductions for state taxes and mortgage interest has shrunk, the standard deduction has grown, making the gap to be filled with charity dollars bigger every year.

After the Republican sweep of Congress and the Presidency in 2024, the Tax Cuts and Jobs Act is likely to be extended past its 2025 expiration date. As Republicans seek to expand its provisions, they will face opposition from Democrats in high-tax states hurt by the SALT cap. The SALT limits may rise in the horse trading for the best overall tax package.

# Capital Gains Tax Avoidance

When you sell stock that has appreciated over the price you paid for it, the proceeds are subject to capital gains taxes. These are typically taxed at lower rates than your ordinary income. A lot of the appreciation in your stocks over time is just inflation, which is itself a kind of tax created by the government's failure to maintain a stable currency. Capital gains taxes are thus a tax upon a tax. Both capital gains and dividend taxes should be adjusted for inflation, but they are not.

If you donate your appreciated stock to a registered public charity, the charity can sell it and pay no taxes because it is a tax-exempt organization. After taxes, a dollar of highly appreciated stock is only worth, say, seventy-six cents to a high earner (and even less after state taxes), but it is worth a full dollar to a public charity. The donor gets a one-dollar deduction—even though twenty-four cents of the dollar they donated would have gone to the government. This discrepancy creates an important charitable-giving opportunity.

These donations appear on Schedule A (as "below-the-line" deductions). They are far more tax-efficient than a gift of an equivalent amount of cash to charity because you get two deductions for the price of one: the immediate income tax deduction this year, as well as avoiding the capital gains taxes that you would have had to pay in the future if you sold the securities.

The size of the benefit depends on how much the securities have appreciated and the brackets at which they would be taxed if sold. If your income is over $250,000 this year, your capital gains tax rate is 20% plus the 3.8% Net Investment Income Tax (added in 2013 to help pay for the Affordable Care Act) for a total of 23.8%. Your state may want to tax these gains as well. In California, you could be taxed up to 13.3% on top of that.

Imagine you donated $16,000 of Apple stock to charity that initially cost you $10,000. If you sold the stock yourself and wrote a check to the charity, you would have to pay $1,428 in federal taxes ($6,000 in gains times the 23.8% capital gains tax rate). You would have paid $16,000 to buy $14,572 worth of charity, making this an expensive gift—not even counting state taxes.

Instead, by donating the stock directly, you flip the script: buying $16,000 worth of charity for what would have been $14,332 after-tax dollars—a much better deal. The charity received the extra cash, and you got to deduct it.

Table 3.1 illustrates this:

| TABLE 3.1: DONATING STOCK VS. SELL & DONATE CASH | | |
|---|---|---|
| | Donate Stock | Donate Cash |
| Stock Cost | $10,000 | $10,000 |
| Stock Current Value | $16,000 | $16,000 |
| Tax on Sale | NA | $1,428 |
| Charitable Donation | $16,000 | $14,572 |
| Standard Deduction | $15,000 | $15,000 |
| **Income Tax Saving** | $240 | $0 |
| **Capital Gains Tax Saving** | $1,428 | $0 |
| **Total Tax Saving** | $1,668 | $0 |

Depending on the situation, sometimes the capital gains tax avoidance will win out, while other times the federal income tax deduction will be more prominent.

Donating appreciated stock is a win-win: you avoid paying unnecessary capital gains taxes, and you get the full benefit for the stock's value as a charitable deduction. Selling the stock and donating the cash is lose-lose: you pay capital gains taxes for no reason, you make a smaller gift to charity as a result, and for all your trouble you get a smaller income tax deduction.

This ability to win two ways makes donating appreciated stock the preferred method of giving to charity for most people, at least preretirement. Later, we will point you to some calcu-lators to help you analyze your situation.

An important exception to this might apply if you were never to sell the stock, and then upon your departure from this dim, vast vale of tears, your shares were to receive a reset to their fair market value, allowing your heirs to sell them and pay no taxes. Of course, we don't know what the government will do in the future. Congress is always threatening to repeal this step-up in cost basis and tax the capital gains at death.

## Testamentary Tax Deductions

When someone passes away, any gifts they make to charity through their estate are exempt from estate taxes. This makes charitable giving at death a popular strategy for wealthy indi-viduals doing last-minute planning to minimize their estate tax liability.

In the absence of estate taxes, a large income tax deduction may be of limited use the year you die. You may not have enough ordinary income to offset it. When made through your will, you receive no income tax benefit at all. It usually would have been more tax-advantageous to make the charitable gift earlier, both to remove the asset and its future growth from your estate as well as to let you take a charitable income tax deduction at the time. The question of giving while living or giving through your estate merits a chinwag with your estate attorney long before checkout time.

Currently, the federal estate tax rate is 40%. However, there is a high exemption amount, meaning that only estates valued over a certain threshold are subject to this tax. In 2025, the exemption will be $13.99 million per individual or $27.98 million for a married couple. If the total value of your estate is less than this amount, you wouldn't owe any federal estate taxes.

However, this historically high exemption is set to expire in 2026. At that point, it is scheduled to revert to around $7.2 million per person. However, the Republican sweep in the 2024 elections makes this drastic fall unlikely.

Sometimes, wealthy donors have burned through their lifetime gift and estate tax exemption by making prior gifts. As a result, any charitable donations they make at death would save 40% on estate taxes. There are also twelve states plus the District of Columbia that impose estate taxes and six states that impose inheritance taxes. I will ignore state taxes because there are fifty states, and their laws are constantly changing. But just because I ignore them does not mean you should. You only have your home state to worry about (and possibly the states where your kids live).

| TABLE 3.2: 2023 STATE ESTATE TAXES AND STATE INHERITANCE TAXES | | | |
|---|---|---|---|
| State | Exemption | Estate Tax | Inheritance Tax |
| Connecticut | $13,610,000 | 12% | |
| Hawaii | $5,490,000 | 10.0% - 20.0% | |
| Illinois | $4,000,000 | 0.8% - 16.0% | |
| Iowa | | | 0-6% |
| Kentucky | | | 0-16% |
| Maine | $6,410,000 | 8.0% - 12.0% | |
| Maryland | $5,000,000 | 0.8% - 16.0% | 0-10% |
| Massachusetts | $2,000,000 | 0.8% - 16.0% | |
| Minnesota | $3,000,000 | 13.0% - 16.0% | |
| Nebraska | | | 0-15% |
| New Jersey | | | 0-16% |
| New York | $6,580,000 | 3.06% - 16.0% | |
| Oregon | $1,000,000 | 10.0%-16.0% | |
| Pennsylvania | | | 0-15% |
| Rhode Island | $1,733,264 | 0.8% - 16.0% | |
| Vermont | $5,000,000 | 16% | |
| Washington | $2,193,000 | 10.0% - 20.0% | |
| District of Columbia | $4,528,800 | 11.2% - 16.0% | |

*Source: Tax Foundation*

If you plan to give via your estate, the place to start is usually with your tax-deferred retirement plans. You want to be specific about which assets to donate, starting with any that contain embedded tax liabilities ("income with respect to a decedent") such as your IRA. You could also name charities as secondary or contingent beneficiaries of these plans. That way, if your children are high-bracket types who will be losing 37% of the IRA withdrawals to taxes anyway, they could disclaim the IRA and send the money to charity instead, which would also lower the estate tax. Your heirs will prefer to receive assets that get a step-up in basis like your brokerage account or the family manor. Specifying which asset goes where is more tax efficient than simply leaving your heirs a percentage of your overall estate.

Table 3.3 illustrates the difference between leaving an IRA vs. a brokerage account to high-bracket heirs vs. to charity. The charity is equally happy either way, but the heirs make out much better with the stepped-up investment portfolio. The presence of Estate Taxes at 40% makes no difference to the choice.

| TABLE 3.3: IRA VS. BROKERAGE TO CHARITY | | | |
|---|---|---|---|
| | IRA to Heirs | Brokerage to Charity | Sum |
| Value of Accounts | $1,000,000 | $1,000,000 | $2,000,000 |
| To Charity | | $1,000,000 | $1,000,000 |
| Estate Tax Saving | $0 | $400,000 | $400,000 |
| Heirs Income Tax Cost | $370,000 | $0 | $370,000 |
| Net to Heirs | $630,000 | $0 | **$630,000** |
| | IRA to Charity | Brokerage to Heirs | Sum |
| Value of Accounts | $1,000,000 | $1,000,000 | $2,000,000 |
| Net to Charity | $1,000,000 | $0 | $1,000,000 |
| Estate Tax Saving | $400,000 | $0 | $400,000 |
| Heirs Income Tax Cost | $0 | $0 | $0 |
| Net to Heirs | $0 | $1,000,000 | **$1,000,000** |

Professor Christopher Hoyt of the University of Missouri Law School recommends putting a clause in your estate plan to this effect:

**Pay Charitable Bequests with IRD and Other Taxable Gross Income**. *Except as otherwise provided in this governing instrument, I instruct my fiduciary that all of my charitable bequests (if any) shall be paid first with taxable income in respect of a decedent (if any), and second with* *any income generated by making the charitable bequest (if any), so that this trust [or estate] shall be entitled to claim a charitable income tax deduction for such transfer under Section 642( c) of The Internal Revenue Code of 1986, as amended, or under any corresponding section of future income tax laws.*

Testamentary gifts can go to a family foundation or a donor-advised fund. Unlike gifts made during life, there is no AGI income cap to worry about; feel free to donate your entire estate if you want. These gifts can even go to foreign charities.

Finally, testamentary gifts are the best way to give if you are at all unsure you have enough money to see you through to your departure. You have every reason to be concerned about running out of money late in life. If you are on the borderline, put the bequest in your will or name a charity as the beneficiary of your retirement plan.

* * *

This chapter has covered the dance card of the most common charitable tax deductions. Now, we will examine how these apply to specific cases.

# Chapter Four

# Giving by
# Cash or Check

## Cash: Wallet-based Philanthropy

Here is a common but expensive use of your charity dollar.

When you give a dollar to someone with his hand out on the street, it costs you a dollar plus the taxes you paid to put that dollar in your wallet. If you are a high earner, that could amount to an extra fifty cents. That would add up to one dollar for the government out of every two dollars you give away—a high tax on personal charity of this type. A less affluent couple might pay 30% in combined Federal and state taxes to give away that dollar: roughly one dollar to the government out of every three they give.

Even if you hand out thousands of dollars from your wallet this way, you will receive no tax benefit because the recipient is not a registered 501(c)(3) public charity.

What about that crisp one-dollar bill you put into the collection plate at church every week? This also costs you the dollar plus your marginal tax rate—unless you document it by sticking it in a numbered envelope that links it to a statement the church sends you to transubstantiate your cash gift into an itemized income tax deduction. But you still might not receive any tax benefit, as we shall see.

## Cash: Checkbook Philanthropy

. . . is a big step up from cash-in-your-pocket charity because now you have a record (in the form of a canceled check) of your donation. This same recordkeeping would apply if you were to use online or digital giving, such as Classy, Givebutter, and Pushpay, among many others.

Even armed with this receipt, your total annual deduction might still be too small to provide you with any economic benefit. A canceled check gives you a leg to stand on with the IRS, but this won't matter until your total deductions surpass the standard deduction. Most people using checkbook philanthropy don't itemize tax deductions on Schedule A of Form 1040. Their charity dollars confer no tax benefit because the total amount of their charitable giving—even when added to their other itemizable deductions—does not exceed the standard deduction. In 2025, the standard deduction comes to $15,000 a year for individuals, while it is $30,000 for those married filing jointly. Seniors over 65 can each add $1,600 to this amount if filing jointly (or $2,000 if filing single).

Until our deductions surpass these amounts, it doesn't matter whether we give cash from our wallet or write a check or if we give the money to a beggar on the street or to a distinguished public charity. Every dollar costs the amount we give plus the federal and state taxes we paid to earn it.

Until the Tax Cuts and Jobs Act expires (and we have no idea what will replace it), the only Schedule A deductions most of us can claim are:

- Up to $10,000 for state and local taxes (including property tax)
- Perhaps $11,000 for a mortgage interest deduction
- Charitable deductions (with further limits to be discussed)
- Medical expenses over 7.5% of adjusted gross income (a high bar I hope you never cross)

Once the abyss of the standard deduction has been filled, the tax benefits a person receives from their next charitable dollar depend on their marginal tax rate.

Here is a rather obvious table showing the tax benefit of a charitable deduction of $100 inside the different tax brackets. State tax savings, if any, would be on top of this.

| TABLE 4.1: FEDERAL TAX DEDUCTIONS | |
|---|---|
| Marginal Tax Rate | Tax Benefit per Itemized $100 Donation |
| 10% | $10 |
| 12% | $12 |
| 15% | $15 |
| 22% | $22 |
| 24% | $24 |
| 32% | $32 |
| 37% | $37 |

People often think that a $100 charitable deduction means you pay $100 less in taxes overall. If that were true, no one would pay taxes. Donating your tax payment to charity would be much more gratifying.

A tax *deduction* is different from a tax *credit. While a tax credit reduces the taxes that you owe dollar-for-dollar, a tax deduction only reduces the amount of your income that will be taxed.* For example, if someone in the 22% tax bracket donates $100 to charity and itemizes deductions eclipsing the standard deduction, they will save $22 in taxes. But had they received a $100 tax credit, they would save $100 in taxes.

Unfortunately, tax credits are hard to find. There is the Earned Income Tax Credit for low-income workers. There is an Adoption Tax Credit for up to $16,810 per child. You can go broke trying to collect tax credits.

While the higher standard deductions under the Tax Cuts and Jobs Act simplify tax filing, they psychologically disincentivize charitable giving from low- and middle-income earners.

## "Bunching" tax deductions

"Bunching" charitable deductions is a tax strategy where you concentrate multiple years' worth of charitable donations into a single tax year to get over the standard deduction by as wide a margin as possible. If you are in the ballpark of the standard deduction but fall short of crossing it, consider whether it would help to make your charitable donations in lumps. If you normally give $10,000 to charity, and instead you decide to give $20,000 one year and $0 the next, you might clear the $15,000/single standard deduction by a wider margin than if you were to give $10,000 every year. You would be making the same net contribution but now on more favorable tax terms.

You can compress your other Schedule A deductions into your charity donation years as well, within limits. For the mortgage interest deduction, you can pay December's (from the previous year) mortgage payment in January and then pay the following December's mortgage payment in December. This would funnel 13 months of mortgage interest into a single calendar year.

There is some leeway for the state and local tax deduction, capped at $10,000 a year. If your county is willing, you might be able to prepay part of next year's property tax this year. Counties are often happy to cash your check today. You can also pay your fourth quarter estimated state income taxes on December 31 this year instead of January 15 next year.

Finally, funnel as many years' worth of charitable contributions as you can into one year. The more your total itemized deductions exceed your standard deduction, the greater the tax advantage to you.

If you are giving to a donor-advised fund, you have the option to parcel out the donations to your end-charities on any timetable you choose. The donor-advised fund is tailor-made for "bunching" contributions since it restores the possibility of a multiyear time spread that you compressed into one year to maximize your tax advantage going in. Christians who tithe will find "bunching" deductions to be the most tax-efficient way to give, since they might collect a tax deduction every two or three years by giving appreciated securities to a donor-advised fund and then parcel out the contributions to their churches annually.

For example, Table 4.2 compares what happens if a single person with a $15,000 standard deduction in the 24% tax bracket gives $50,000 to charity in one year rather than giving $10,000 to charity every year for five years. The moral: go big, less often. At the same time, you have to be aware that your charitable tax deduction is not unlimited: when bunching, you need to stay under the "percentage of adjusted gross income limits" discussed at the end of this chapter.

| TABLE 4.2: BUNCHING CHARITABLE DEDUCTIONS - 24% TAX BRACKET | | | |
|---|---|---|---|
| Donation | Total Charitable Donation | Tax Deduction | Tax Savings |
| $50,000 in one year | $50,000 | $35,000 | $8,400 |
| $10,000/year for five years | $50,000 | $0 | $0 |

This works best when you have a running start on the standard deduction from your state and local taxes and mortgage interest. Did your husband break his leg skiing in Gstaad and require a hugely expensive medivac? Your thoughts should immediately go to listing the expense on Schedule A. Absent other deductions, it is hard to get much traction from bunching if the first $30,000 of your gift (married filing jointly) is swallowed by the standard deduction, especially without crashing into the AGI limits (exceeding 60% of your adjusted gross income if donating cash or 30% of your adjusted gross income if donating securities). Alas, just because the deduction would be super desirable in your situation does not mean that it will be available. Many people will not be able to make bunching deductions help very much under the current high standard deduction, although it still may be the best avenue open to them.

Bunching deductions takes a certain amount of work to optimize.

## "Bunching" Checklist

- Add up your current Schedule A itemized deductions, including medical expenses over 7.5% of adjusted gross income, charity, mortgage interest, and state and local taxes

- How close does this bring you to the $15,000 single/$30,000 married filing jointly standard deduction? If doubling or tripling your charitable deduction would put you over the standard deduction, you would be a candidate for bunching your deductions into every other or every third year

- Verify that your enlarged charitable donation during the "bunched" year does not exceed your Adjusted Gross Income limitations: typically 60% of AGI if all cash or 50% of AGI if a combination of cash plus securities
- Your tax saving from bunching should roughly equal the amount you exceed the standard deduction multiplied by your marginal tax rate. Is it worth the extra effort?
- Consider opening a Donor-Advised Fund if your goal is to give to charity annually but bunch donations for tax purposes intermittently
- If donating every other year, consider paying January's mortgage in December, prepaying property taxes, and paying Q4 estimated state taxes in December instead of January for the targeted "bunched" year
- If donating securities is envisioned, scan your portfolio for the best candidates to donate (see the next chapter for more on this)
- Run the idea by your tax professionals
- Review your tax return after the "bunched" year to see whether it worked as intended
- Take the standard deduction in the off years

# Employer Matching Gifts

If you work for a large public corporation—especially a technology company or a financial services firm—you might have an employer match available to leverage your charitable giving as part of your benefit package. You might even have a corporate match available if you work for a small company, although it is less likely. This is potentially an outstanding way to leverage your giving and may turn out to be the best charity deal you will ever see.

Any percentage match offered is worth investigating. Since matches are frequently 100%—in other words, 1:1, dollar-for-dollar—these leverage your gift even though you can't itemize the corporation's share of the contribution on your income tax.

Let's say you can give $100 to charity, and it costs you $115 to give it after taxes because you are in the 15% tax bracket. That seems like a bad deal. But if you can get a matching gift from your employer, then you are effectively giving $200 to charity for $115. This is a terrific deal.

If your employer offers a matching gift, contact your Human Resources department and thoroughly investigate the terms. The devil is in the details:

- Are you eligible? It might be available to all employees and even to retirees, but in most cases it will be limited to current full-time employees only.

- What is the ratio of the match? Most companies offer a dollar-for-dollar match, but some might offer less while others will pay more. The best case is if you work for the Ford Foundation, which makes a 3:1 match up to a limit of $30,000. You can give $30,000 to charity and the Ford Foundation promotes you to philanthropist status, with a $120,000 donation in all.
- How much? The benefit is never unlimited. It will extend over some range, like gifts from $25 to $1,000.
- Which charities are eligible? In the best case, all 501(c)(3) charities make the cut. Religious charities are often excluded. Giving to your own Donor-Advised Fund or Private Foundation probably will not work either. Sometimes the charities are winnowed down to a short list—either local charities, or charities related to the company's business mission.
- What is the drill? Do you have to submit a paper form to claim the match? If so, examine it to see what you are in for. Increasingly, matches are managed online at the charity's end. In that case, your company is automatically notified when you flag them as you make your own gift.
- Can you make the gift from your Donor-Advised Fund? While you will get no further charitable deduction for a

gift from your DAF, you will be able to leverage the gift through the employer match on top of any tax deduction you received when you opened your DAF in the first place. This combination can be powerful.

Your contemporary written acknowledgment from the charity will specify your direct contribution only. The company will take its own tax deduction, which is a big part of the reason the matching program exists.

# Rules:

Did I mention that getting credit for your charitable donations requires assiduously following complicated rules? As you read these over, ignore anything that does not apply to you. Do not assume that, because you give to charity, the IRS will be understanding about any errors you make. On the contrary, they will be relentless and merciless.

If you mail a check to a charity, the date of the contribution for tax purposes is the day you mail it. You will not be able to prove this unless you send the check by certified mail, which might mean standing in line at the post office for an hour around Christmas to get a receipt. While large charities do an outstanding job of cashing your checks (whales swallowing plankton), this task can take small charities an inordinate amount of time. A client reported a case where she mailed her check on November 15, but the charity did not bother cashing it until January 3 the following year. The taxpayer had no recourse. She assumed the charity would cash her check before year-end. If you have not heard from your charity by mid-December, call them to investigate while there is still time to solve the problem.

Figure 4.1 shows the fascinating portion of Schedule A where your tax form presents your gifts to charity:

**FIGURE 4.1:**
## Schedule A: Gifts to Charity

| Gifts to Charity | 11 | Gifts by cash or check. If you made any gift of $250 or more, see instructions . . . . . . . . . . . . . . . . . . . . . . . . . . | 11 | |
|---|---|---|---|---|
| Caution: If you made a gift and got a benefit for it, see instructions. | 12 | Other than by cash or check. If you made any gift of $250 or more, see instructions. You **must** attach Form 8283 if over $500 . . . . | 12 | |
| | 13 | Carryover from prior year . . . . . . . . . . . . . . . | 13 | |
| | 14 | Add lines 11 through 13 . . . . . . . . . . . . . . . . . . . . . . . . . | | 14 |

A cash gift of less than $250 to a charity (Schedule A, Line 11) has no substantiation requirements. If you put $5 in the collection plate at church for fifty-two Sundays last year, you would have donated (52 X $5) $260 in total. That would still go on Line 11, even though the amount is over $250. Why? Because each donation was under $250. The IRS views each $5 as a separate charitable gift.

To say there are no specific substantiation requirements is not to say that the IRS cannot disallow the deduction if they do not believe you. If you are audited, it will be comforting to have a canceled check and a letter from the charity to show them. But there are no formal requirements.

This changes once you make any gift to charity over $250 (the next line, Schedule A, Line 12). Now you need a *contemporaneous written acknowledgment* from the charity. "Contemporaneous" here means by the time the tax return (including any extension period) is due. This written acknowledgment is not submitted with your tax return but is kept with your records in case you are audited later. It includes:

- the name of the charity
- the date of the donation
- the dollar amount
- A stipulation that no goods or services were provided in exchange for your gift
- Or, if goods or services were provided to you, the charity's good faith estimate of their value
- For donations such as closely held company stock, a stipulation that the charity has total discretion and control over the shares and can retain or sell them as it chooses

While not specifically called for, even better would be:

- The immediate source of the donation: An IRA? A trust? An individual? Details, please
- The date they received the check
- The check number

This does not have to be on paper. It can be an email.

If you are audited, the easiest way for the IRS examiner to make money is by asking to see the contemporaneous written acknowledgment for your charitable donation. Chances are you either won't be able to find it, or it will not be in good order. Then your deduction will be denied, no matter what the amount, with no remedy, and the money moved back to the taxable income column. You have just paid for your own audit.

If you receive any material benefit (food, entertainment, tickets, swag) in exchange for your gift, its value counts against your deduction. The whole transaction might be regarded with suspicion. You should be okay if you get a smile, a hearty hand-clasp, and a pat on the back from a development officer. If, additionally, they offer you a toothpick, a glass of water, and a plastic ballpoint pen with the charity's name on it, you should still pass inspection. Beyond this, be careful. When you sign your tax return, you are declaring under penalty of perjury that the return is true, correct, and complete. That's how the IRS nailed Al Capone.

While I would argue that someone who donates money to his college for priority access to football tickets receives a benefit of a purely spiritual nature, team IRS disagrees: this deduction is expressly disallowed. The agency has also determined that paying a college athlete is not a charitable purpose, even if the athlete does some charitable work on the side. It's not always easy doing good.

Back to Schedule A:

Line 12 – Gifts of property. The subject of the next chapter.

Line 13 – What is this about a carryover from the prior year? Let me explain. . .

## Adjusted Gross Income Limitations

The IRS limits how much you can deduct from your taxes for charitable contributions in any one year. It tops out at 60% of your Adjusted Gross Income (AGI). You will recall that your AGI is your total income but excludes such niceties as Individual Retirement Account (IRA) and Health Savings Account (HSA) contributions, some educational expenses, alimony, and various business expenses for the self-employed.

*If you have an adjusted gross income of $100,000, the most you can deduct for giving to a public charity is 60% in cash.* While there are many things to worry about in life, the fear of giving to charity past this limit is not one of them for most people—although for some people, it is. The 60% limit is slated to drop back to 50% if the Tax Cuts and Jobs Act expires at the end of 2025.

*For cash donations to private foundations, the limit is 30% of your adjusted gross income.* If you have an AGI of $100,000, you can deduct a maximum of 30% or $30,000 in cash for charitable contributions to the private foundation.

*If you are giving long-term (> 1 year) appreciated property like stocks or real estate to a public charity, you can give up to 30% of AGI,* or $30,000 in this example. If you are donating art, you are limited to its cost basis, unless the art is relevant to the charity's mission, in which case you can use fair market value, as discussed later.

*If you are giving long-term appreciated property like stocks or real estate to a private (non-operating) foundation, you can give up to 20% of AGI,* or $20,000 in this example.

*If you are giving your private company stock to your private (nonoperating) foundation, you are limited to a total cumulative gift of 20% of your adjusted gross income. This only applies to your cost basis in the stock or its fair market value, whichever is less.* The same limits apply when donating tangible personal property such as art to your foundation: appreciation does not count.

If you donate publicly traded stock to your private foundation or donate real estate or tangible personal property to a public charity, you will get a deduction for their fair market value (although AGI limits still apply). The big idea is that the tax code intentionally favors donating cash over stock and property, and favors donating to public charities over private foundations.

There is a stacking order governing how these contributions can be combined:

- Cash contributions (up to 60% of AGI) to these organizations are taken first
- Noncash contributions (stocks, real estate, appreciated property) to public charities, DAFs, and private *operating* foundations, up to the 30% of AGI limit
- Cash contributions to private (non-operating) foundations, subject to the 30% of AGI limit
- Noncash contributions to private foundations, subject to the 20% of AGI limit

But – *if stocks and cash are both given to charity, the stacking rules say the total combined percentage of AGI drops from 60% to 50%. The 60% limit is for donations exclusively of cash.* If the donations are of cash in combination with anything else, the combined AGI limit is 50%. The cash gift is counted first, and will crowd out all the other components of the deduction if the cash gift is over 20% (to a public charity) or over 30% (to a private foundation).

For example, John has an AGI of $100,000:

- He donates $30,000 in cash to a public charity (against 60% AGI limit)
- He donates $20,000 in public securities to his private foundation (against 20% AGI limit)
- He can deduct both donations from his taxes
- His total tax deduction for charitable contributions is $50,000, the maximum allowed for a combined stock + cash donation

You can give away any amount of money you want. However, only 60% of your adjusted gross income will be eligible for a cash tax deduction. The most you could give to a DAF in appreciated securities for a deduction is 30% of AGI in any one year.

If you give away more than this, there is still hope. You can carry forward the remainder on Line 13 of Schedule A (see figure 4.1) for up to five years following. But you will have to keep track of this amount, and in each of the five years it will be subject to the same AGI limits tests that it faced originally.

For example, John has an adjusted gross income of $100,000:

- In an extravagant mood, he gives all $100,000 in cash to a public charity. Because of the 60% limit, he can only claim $60,000 as a charitable deduction that year.

- This leaves him with a $40,000 charitable deduction he can carry forward for the next five years.

- The following year, John retires. He does not start Social Security or take distributions from his IRA. He has no income. Because 60% of zero equals zero, he cannot deduct any of the remaining $40,000 that year.

- Seeing the error of his ways, the next year, John withdraws $100,000 from his IRA, giving him an AGI of $100,000.

- Since the $40,000 charitable contribution is still within the 5-year window, and because it is under 60% of his $100,000 AGI, John can take a charitable deduction for the entire $40,000 remainder this year.

Notice that spreading out the donation over five years otherwise confers no tax advantage over taking the entire deduction in year one because each year your charitable deduction faces the standard deduction hurdle and will be trimmed by inflation. There may be cases where this is the least bad strategy, but there is no reason to seek out the opportunity for its own sake.

If you plan on giving different assets to different types of charities, or if you are giving appreciated personal property or shares in a closely held business, or are concerned you might be brushing up against AGI limits, your first call should be to your accountant to get their blessing. As Davy Crockett would say, "Be sure you're right—then go ahead."

Finally, if you choose to give via your estate, you can skip all the AGI income limitations.

Chapter Five

# Donating **Securities**

The most tax-efficient way for most people to give to charity is by using appreciated publicly traded securities from their taxable brokerage accounts: stocks, bonds, REITs, mutual funds, exchange-traded funds, etc. As we saw back in Chapter Three, donating appreciated stock gives you a double deduction: first, you can claim an income tax deduction for their full market value, and second, you avoid the capital gains taxes you would have had to pay on the securities had you sold them yourself. The government is giving you a deduction for the full (pretax) value of the securities, even though they were only worth their posttax value to you.

Give the stock directly to the charity and let the charity sell it. That way, the sale will be tax-exempt, the charity will receive the proceeds tax-free, and you will get a deduction for the full pretax amount.

# Checklist for Donating Securities to Charity

- Run the idea by your tax advisors
- Contact the 501(c)(3) charity you wish to give to and obtain the name and address of their brokerage firm where they receive security donations, the name and account number of the charity's brokerage account, and their DTC (Depository Trust Company) number
- Review your brokerage account for the best securities to donate (more on this later): name, symbol, number of shares, date(s) acquired, cost basis
- Verify that this donation will not exceed the 30% AGI percentage-of-income limits as discussed in the last chapter
- Contact your broker and tell them you want to initiate a broker-to-broker transfer of securities to a charity. They will almost certainly direct you to the forms library where you can download a Letter of Authorization specifying the details of the transfer
- You will enter all the above information in the appropriate boxes on this form and upload it for their execution

- Keep a record of the value of the stock on the day it was irretrievably sent: typically, this is the price halfway between the high and low prices for the day

- The transfer will go through the Automated Customer Account Transfer Service (ACATS) and will take 3-5 business days (but possibly longer at year-end)

- Follow up to make sure the transfer was completed successfully

- Get the letter of acknowledgment from the charity detailing the gift

- Report the donation on Schedule A and File Form 8283 Section A for noncash charitable contributions over $500

This is about as much fun as it looks.

The easy way to do this is to seamlessly move the securities from your (Vanguard/Fidelity/Schwab) brokerage account directly to your (Vanguard/Fidelity/Schwab) donor-advised fund with a few points and clicks on the DAF website. The DAF will immediately grab them, sell them, and give you credit for the full dollar value of your donation. If you can "bunch" these donations into a single tax year (as discussed in the last chapter) it would be even better. DAFs also will be advantageous if your goal is to use appreciated stock to make smaller contributions to multiple end charities over time, since many small charities are not equipped to handle donated securities. This way, there will be only one charitable donation to report on your Schedule A: the one from your brokerage account to your DAF. They even make the tax paperwork and security selection process easy. Once you have tried it, you won't go back to the old way.

## Which shares to donate?

The best stock to send to the charity is usually the one with your lowest cost basis, which means the highest embedded capital gains. *This may not be obvious from scanning your brokerage statement because you may have purchased the same stock, mutual fund or exchange-traded fund over time at different prices, while your statement might only show the average cost you paid.* Drill down another level into your positions and tell the brokerage to send the charity the specific lowest-basis shares you have hand-picked. Identify the number of shares, the date they were acquired, and the price paid.

That way, the charity gets the $10,000 in Apple shares you bought long ago for $1,000 and pays no capital gains on the $9,000 of capital appreciation while you get the full $10,000 tax deduction. Meanwhile, you retain the other $10,000 in Apple shares you bought last year for $9,000, on which your gain would only be $1,000 if you had to sell them.

A second category to donate is dividend-paying stocks. Tax-wise, a dividend is equivalent to a capital gain that has a zero-cost basis. Dividend stocks are fine in IRAs because the dividends are taxed as ordinary income when distributed to you, the same as capital gains. But in a brokerage account the extra taxes on dividends amount to a self-inflicted carrying charge.

Table 5.1 shows the trade-offs between donating securities with capital gains vs. securities that pay dividends. If you donate a stock with high capital gains to charity, the one-time tax savings can be high (as in the top row). On the other hand, if you donate a high-dividend-paying stock to charity, the tax savings are low, but they recur every year.

| TABLE 5.1: Sample Capital Gains vs. Dividends | | | |
|---|---|---|---|
| $10,000 Stock | | @ 15% Tax | @ 23.8% Tax |
| Cost Basis | Capital Gains | Tax Savings | Tax Savings |
| $1,000 | $9,000 | $1,350 | $2,142 |
| $5,000 | $5,000 | $750 | $1,190 |
| $8,000 | $2,000 | $300 | $476 |

| Dividend Yield | Annual Dividend $ | Annual Tax Savings | Annual Tax Savings |
|----------------|-------------------|---------------------|---------------------|
| 1% | $100 | $15 | $24 |
| 2% | $200 | $30 | $48 |
| 3% | $300 | $45 | $71 |
| 4% | $400 | $60 | $95 |

As a rule of thumb, look first to stocks or mutual funds with the lowest cost basis/highest embedded capital gains to give to charity, and from there select the stocks paying the highest dividends because these have the highest holding cost for you. The exception would be if you anticipate never having to sell the low-basis stock and can leave it to your heirs with a step-up in basis. In practice, the low-basis stock would be the last shares you would sell because they are the most tax-expensive to liquidate. In that case, start with the high-dividend stocks, which have the highest carrying cost for you.

Other investments to ditch would be the old mutual funds with high expense ratios and poor tax efficiency (which often go hand in hand). Mutual funds are much worse than individual stocks and exchange-traded funds (ETFs) because they have mandatory payouts of their capital gains every year for your tax-paying pleasure. In a big down year for the stock market, fleeing shareholders force the fund to redeem stocks to buy them out, leaving the remaining loyal buy-and-hold shareholders with a big bill for the resulting capital gains taxes. This isn't fair, but that's how it works.

So-called "collectibles" like shares in precious-metal funds (such as GLD or IAU) would also be good to give away since they are taxed at 28% instead of 15% or 20%.

With crackerjack financial advisors, or even on your own, you can carefully manage your charitable giving to maximize your tax advantage every year, fine-tuning your ordinary income to stay under the various thresholds where higher taxes or Medicare premium surcharges start to bite.

Donating the stocks and funds that are the most expensive for you to hold (high dividend yields, high expense ratios) or sell (large, long-term capital gains) means the stocks remaining in your portfolio will be cheaper to hold and sell. This is a win-win situation for you and the charity.

One final consideration: other things equal, give away stocks you can lose without doing undue violence to your overall asset allocation.

## Rules:

If you are donating stock, the effective date is the date your brokerage firm transfers the title or the date you can prove you permanently relinquished dominion and control over the security (i.e., you were unable to change your mind and call it back).

In the unlikely event you are delivering a paper stock certificate, the effective date is when it was delivered, properly endorsed, to the agent of the charitable organization. If this certificate is mailed, it is the date you mailed it (retain proof). If you give a stock certificate to your broker to transfer to the charity, the date of the contribution is the date it lands on the books of the receiving corporation.

Don't postpone this until the end of December when everyone on Wall Street is at that disco on St. Bart's, or your plan could backfire. Give your brokerage plenty of time to ship the securities out. If your broker fails to get them to the charity on time despite "best efforts," it is your problem, not theirs.

Unlike cash, deductions for gifts of stock to a public charity are limited to 30% of your adjusted gross income (although you can top off your donation with cash for a total combined limit of 50%—not 60% as when you were donating cash alone). You can also carry forward any unused deduction for five years, but this will be wasted if you are "bunching" deductions.

You can give any amount you wish through your estate, although that is not usually the best strategy.

As mentioned in the last chapter, if you are giving publicly traded stock to your own private foundation, you are limited to a deduction of 20% of your adjusted gross income. On top of this, you can give cash to your private foundation up to a combined total of 30% of adjusted gross income.

Finally, *all capital gains donated to charity must be long-term to secure a tax deduction.* You must have held the shares you are donating for more than one year to get the benefit from capital gains avoidance.

## Donating shares of your Private Company

Your private company or family business is probably a Limited Liability Company, a Limited Partnership, a C corporation, or an S corporation. It might also be a holding in your Family LLC or LP. You might be making a charitable gift to a public charity or your own private, nonoperating foundation. But if you have Qualified Small Business Stock, there is no point in donating these shares to charity because QSBS is already tax-exempt.

If you want to donate your closely held company stock to a public charity, you will need a qualified independent appraisal from a qualified appraiser for any donation over $10,000. If you give away a portion of your private company, the IRS will apply a discount to your tax deduction due to a lack of marketability and control for a minority interest in the business. You might use 10% as a first approximation, but ultimately this will have to be justified by an empirically based calculation.

You will also need to find a charity willing to accept it. Most public charities are not set up to receive "Unrelated Business Income" from your operating business, so they don't want private stock unless a sale where they will cash out is imminent. A donor-advised fund would be a good candidate.

The play goes like this: A shareholder gives appreciated shares of the closely held C corporation, LLC, or partnership interest to a public charity. The charitable deduction is claimed based on the discounted value of these shares in the qualified appraisal of the fair market value of the business. Then the C corporation, LLC, or partnership offers to buy the shares back from the charity for a cash amount equal to the same discounted value. The charity—under no legal obligation or coercion but acting out of enlightened self-interest (perhaps per an informal understanding with the donor)—chooses to sell the shares back to the business. As law professor Christopher Hoyt puts it, "The *shareholder* can claim a charitable tax deduction for the gift of appreciated property, but it is the *corporation's cash* that ultimately goes to the charity."

The S corporation is more complicated. The tax deduction received would be less than the appraised value, and a charity is not a qualified S corporation shareholder. The workaround is for an S corporation to donate cash directly to the charity. Because the S corporation is a pass-through entity, this donation flows directly through to the owner's tax return via Form K-1, where it would be listed as a Schedule A charitable deduction. If this can't work for some reason, there is an outfit called Charitable Solutions LLC in Jacksonville, Florida, that can facilitate donating S corporation stock. They consult with both the donor and the charity to make the transfer tax-efficiently.

There was a recent case (Hoensheid, 2023) where a business owner gave shares of his private business to a donor-advised fund but waited until just before the sale to make the donation. After all, what if the sale fell through? It seemed sensible to wait. But the IRS argued, and the judge agreed, that since by that time he already knew the sale price, this amounted to "assignment of income"—the splitting of income among people or entities for the sole purpose of avoiding taxation, a no-no. As a result of this ruling, he owed capital gains taxes on the zero-basis stock he contributed. He then claimed a deduction for the charitable gift. Except—the court said he couldn't do that either because the qualified appraisal was inadequate. He didn't think he needed a stellar appraisal because he already knew the price his company was going to sell for. This case underscores the necessity of working closely with your legal and tax advisors when it comes to donating shares of a family business or privately held company to charity.

# Chapter Six

# Retirement Account
# **Philanthropy**

*"The best time to plant a tree was twenty years ago."*

- CHINESE PROVERB

Most married people with Traditional IRAs make their spouse the primary beneficiary and their kids secondary or contingent beneficiaries who will inherit the account after their surviving spouse goes to heaven.

But when this surviving spouse dies, the IRA will face a number of obstacles. The first is the estate tax. In 2025, the 40% estate tax threshold is high: $13.99 million, but it may change in 2026. Sen. Bernie Sanders thinks this should be lowered to $3.5 million. Some states will also levy an inheritance or gift tax on your beneficiaries when they receive the money.

The problem with Traditional IRAs is that they hold pretax dollars. IRAs gave you a nice tax deduction during your working years while you were funding the accounts, but that was yesterday. They receive no step-up in cost basis when their owner dies. Now, they contain what accountants call "income in respect of a decedent," which represents a large unpaid tax bill. Their distributions will be taxed as ordinary income.

Thanks to the SECURE Act, in nearly all cases, your kids will be forced to pull all the money out of your IRA over ten years. These big withdrawals of ordinary income are designed to maximize taxation (with penalties as high as 25% if they make mistakes while trying to follow the bewildering, ever-changing rules).

While, in theory, your heirs might receive partial credit for any estate tax that was paid on their share of the IRA, they will only get this if they are tax-savvy, compulsive recordkeepers. This often fails because the accountant who settles the estate is not the same accountant who prepares the kids' tax returns, so the vital tax information gets lost.

If you have charitable intentions, and your heirs don't need the money, the Traditional IRA is the first asset to consider donating to charity. The charity will never have to pay the tax bill. It sells the assets and receives one hundred cents on the dollar, while your human beneficiaries would have to pay taxes on these same distributions at their ordinary income tax rates.

There are two possibilities here, and both can be tax efficient. You can give this money away via a Qualified Charitable Distribution during your lifetime, or you can give some or all of it to charity after you die by using your IRA account beneficiary forms.

Note: Some people own "self-directed" IRAs, which are required when using an IRA to hold "alternative" assets (real estate, precious metals, private equity, etc.) not available in standard retirement plans. Self-directed IRAs can be used for charitable giving along the lines described in this chapter, but the process is more complicated. The first place to stop for advice would be your self-directed IRA custodian, and then loop in your accountant or attorney as needed.

## Qualified Charitable Distributions (QCDs)

Taxpayers over the age of 70½ can direct their IRA custodian to donate up to $108,000 from a Traditional or Inherited IRA. QCDs are a foundational concept for tax-efficient charitable giving.

Your QCD will count against the IRA's Required Minimum Distribution (RMD) for the year. While technically you can begin giving QCDs at age 70½, you will receive no immediate tax benefit if you take a QCD before your RMDs start at age 73 (although technically you would get a small tax benefit because pre-RMD QCDs would lower the IRA balance used to calculate future RMDs).

For most of us, the RMD at age 73 will be well below $108,000. A million-dollar IRA at retirement might only ramp up to a $108,000 annual RMD by the time the owner reaches their nineties. A 73-year-old would need an IRA balance of about $4,000,000 to require a distribution that large. This $108,000-to-charity limit is indexed for inflation and will go up over time.

The donation does not need to be for the full RMD to receive a tax benefit; it can be for any amount up to the RMD figure. While you can give up to $108,000 in 2025, you will receive no tax benefit from giving any amount greater than your RMD.

A QCD applied against an RMD has important advantages:

- While the donor does not get a Schedule A charitable tax deduction, they get a much better deal: the QCD is excluded from their adjusted gross income just like an "above-the-line" deduction
- It may also help taxpayers avoid the 3.8% Net Investment Income Tax

- The QCD lowers the threshold for deducting medical care expenses and possibly your Medicare Income-Related Monthly Adjustment Amount (IRMAA) surtax
- The QCD opens a backdoor to lowering state income taxes for residents of states that do not allow charitable tax deductions
- The QCD will not be swallowed by the standard deduction, which can be especially useful to retirees who might no longer claim a Schedule A home mortgage deduction
- QCDs do not count against any of the percentage-of-income limits on charitable donations discussed earlier – you can give away the QCD on top of those full amounts if you wish

Donors over 70½ who want to give away more than the QCD maximum of $108,000 a year can supplement it with gifts of cash or appreciated stock to charity, up to statutory limits.

The QCD leverages your dollar donation (up to the RMD amount) by your marginal tax rate. If you are in the 15% bracket, you buy a dollar of charity for 85 cents. In the 35% bracket, you buy a dollar of charity for 65 cents.

Effectively, the ability to make QCDs transforms your humble IRA into a private charitable foundation operating with pretax dollars. This can make QCDs the first choice for charity for those who have started taking RMDs. The biggest winners from this strategy will be the 90% of people who rely on the standard deduction (i.e., who don't itemize deductions on Schedule A) as well as those who live in states that don't allow charitable deductions on their state income tax (to be discussed shortly).

You can combine a QCD with a regular IRA withdrawal to satisfy your overall RMD that year. What you want to avoid above all is withdrawing money from your IRA, paying taxes on it at your marginal rate, and then sending these after-tax proceeds to charity, since by using a QCD, that money could have gone directly to charity tax-free.

The convenience of sending out a QCD depends on your IRA custodian. In some cases, tedious paperwork is required. Custodians are aware of how easy it is for seniors to screw up their IRA withdrawals as well as the extortionate IRS penalties for mistakes, so they try to keep the guardrails up. But once you hit age 70, many of them will relent and issue you a checkbook on your IRA if you ask for one. *The name of the charity must be the payee on your check.* Never touch the money yourself.

## Rules

QCDs cannot be made from employer plans like 401(k), 403(b), or 457 plans. Roll these over to an IRA if you want to make QCDs.

A SEP IRA still being used to receive contributions cannot make a QCD.

A SIMPLE IRA still being used to make contributions cannot make a QCD until two further years have passed.

While technically a Roth IRA could be used, it should not be, since you would be giving the charity expensive posttax dollars.

A Traditional or Inherited IRA can and should be used, provided all the money in is pretax. If you have commingled pre- and posttax funds inside your IRA, this becomes astonishingly complicated, so ask your accountant what to do.

A QCD must go directly to a public 501(c)(3) registered charity and never to a donor-advised fund, a private nonoperating foundation, or a supporting organization.

You must take out all QCDs BEFORE pulling out your RMD for the year. For the IRS, the first money out of your IRA every year is your RMD, no matter what you might call it. The new rule of thumb is to take QCDs in January and any remaining RMD in December (for an extra eleven months of tax-free compounding).

Per usual, you need the standard contemporaneous written acknowledgment from the charity saying you received nothing of value in exchange for your contribution. You don't submit this with your taxes but file away it in case you are audited later.

*Attention! There is no box on Form 1040 to let you enter the QCD, and there never will be.* The IRS asks you to report the full amount of your withdrawal on Form 1040 on line 4a. Then, on line 4b, show the total distribution minus the QCD and write "QCD" next to it. Your accountant knows how to do this, but *you need to tell them specifically about your QCDs because it is not called out anywhere on the IRA's Form 1099-R on their desk.*

The QCD is problematic for anyone who worked past age $70\frac{1}{2}$ and continued to contribute to their IRA. For unknown reasons, Congress was concerned a person might earn money during retirement, make IRA contributions for a deduction from their income tax, and then do a QCD on top of it, further lowering their income that year.

As a result, you can't start taking QCDs until you have pulled out and paid taxes on an amount equal to *all* your post-$70\frac{1}{2}$ IRA contributions. You will reach this breakeven at some point after you retire, but you (or your accountant) will have to calculate exactly when.

Here is a workaround:

Married couples can pay taxes on a joint basis, but Individual Retirement Accounts remain forever "individual." One partner can work and make post-$70\frac{1}{2}$ contributions to their IRA, while the other who does not could take the QCDs from their IRA. These would be netted on the joint tax return, all perfectly legit.

# QCD Checklist

For maximum tax advantage:

- You are 73 or over and have not made deposits to your IRA since you began taking RMDs
- You have a Traditional or an Inherited IRA and have not commingled pre- and posttax dollars inside the account
- You have not yet taken your RMD this year
- The amount of the QCD is equal to or less than your RMD
- The amount of the QCD is equal to or less than $108,000 (for 2025)
- Your proposed charity is not a donor-advised fund, a nonoperating private foundation, or a supporting organization
- Your check, which is either from your IRA custodian or your IRA checkbook, is payable directly to the charity, and you will track down the acknowledgment letter from them for your records
- You will remember to tell your tax preparer about your QCD

# State Taxes

Let's take a road trip to see how QCDs interact with state taxes.

Most states follow the federal approach and so will let you exclude the entire QCD amount. However, there is no necessary synchronization between federal and state treatment of retirement income. In the worst case, for example, New Jersey does not follow the federal tax code and will tax you on all distributions from your IRA, including on a QCD.

The following states accept the federal AGI as their starting point, even though they offer no deduction for charitable donations on their state taxes. They will specifically exclude any below-the-line charitable deductions you claim on your federal Schedule A:

- Connecticut
- Indiana
- Michigan
- New Jersey
- Ohio
- Pennsylvania
- West Virginia

For these states, QCDs offer a *de facto* charitable state tax deduction that cannot be obtained in any other way. If you live in

Ohio and write a check to the Sierra Club, you get no tax deduction from your Ohio taxes. But if you give a QCD to the Sierra Club, you reduce your Ohio taxable income by that amount.

The QCD is irrelevant for states that do not charge an income tax, as well as for Pennsylvania, which has an income tax but does not tax IRA distributions.

## State Tax Credits

Here we are getting deep into the weeds.

When the Tax Cuts and Jobs Act was passed in 2017, a howl went up from the rich, high-tax coastal blue states. The bill capped the deduction for state and local taxes at $10,000. Previously, residents could deduct their entire state tax bill—even a 6-figure amount—from their federal taxes.

In protest, their liberal state legislatures came up with a loophole: let their citizens contribute to specially designated in-state charities and then give them credit for it against their state income tax. This offered salvation: if their state tax bill was $60,000, a resident might donate $50,000 to a local homeless shelter, get credit for that against their state tax bill, and pay the final $10,000 owed to the state. They would deduct the $10,000—the maximum allowed—as state tax from their federal taxes and claim the $50,000 as a charitable tax deduction against their federal taxes on Schedule A.

The IRS correctly ruled that this violated the intent of the law. Since the state residents received $50,000 of economic benefit in the form of state tax savings from their "charitable" donation, it could not be claimed as a tax deduction on Schedule A of their federal tax return.

The states lost. But in some states, there remains a shrunken vestigial appendage of this loophole that still works.

Let's walk through the pros and cons using an example from Arizona. Something similar might apply in your state.

Here is the loophole we will be exploiting:

Will the IRS ever, under any circumstances, let you deduct the QCD for which you received a state tax credit on Schedule A of your Federal Income Tax?

Yes. . . *provided the state tax credit is less than 15% of the QCD.*

Arizona offers a credit of $400 single/$800 married against state income tax for donations to their designated charities.

If an Arizona couple made a $1,000 QCD to a designated charity, what would happen? Because the tax credit ($800) comprises fully 80% of the QCD ($1,000), the QCD fails the test (set by the IRS at 15%).

Let's change the numbers and try again.

If the Arizona couple made a $5,335 QCD to the same eligible charity, the Arizona tax credit still would be $800. Now, it (just) flies under the 15%-of-the-QCD threshold. The taxpayer would get the full Arizona $800 tax credit, plus the entire QCD would stand, such that $5,335 would disappear from their adjusted gross income. Per usual, the taxpayers could not claim a tax deduction, since the donation came from an IRA and appears "above the line." If the taxpayers had other deductions and wanted to itemize them, they would have to add back an $800 state tax credit on Schedule A. But if they settle for the standard deduction and do not itemize, they have their cake and eat it too: the $800 state tax credit plus $5,335 subtracted from AGI on their federal taxes.

All this assumes you love the state charity in question. If you don't find a state charity you love, it's not worth buying something you don't want simply because it is cheap.

With the caveat that states are always changing their tax policies, here is a list of states that offer state tax credits in exchange for charitable contributions.

- Arizona
- Indiana
- Iowa
- Mississippi
- Montana

- Ohio
- South Carolina

By the time you read this, your home state may have joined this list—or fallen off. Look up your state's tax credits, read the fine print, and follow the rules. Run the strategy by your tax advisors before attempting the QCD + state tax credit combo platter.

## Leaving your IRA to a Charity Beneficiary

This is another key idea for tax-effective charitable planning. Your retirement plans—IRAs, 401(k)s, 403(b)s, etc. do not pass through your estate at all. Your will might say to leave your IRA to your nephew Cecil, but this will be ignored. Your IRA will go to whomever you specified on the IRA plan paperwork. If the plan paperwork names Fred, it won't go to Cecil, no matter what your will says.

Attorneys sometimes draft IRA beneficiary designations, and in certain cases this may be necessary. Most of the time, the beneficiary designation forms from the major IRA and 401(k) providers work better. They are simple to fill out and simple for the custodians to understand and follow without the red tape

and delay of funneling everything through their legal departments. These retirement plan beneficiary designations should
be integrated into your estate plan.

Here is the single best piece of advice in this book: drop
everything right now, look up each of your retirement accounts
online, and verify that the named beneficiaries are exactly as
you intend. For example, your new bride may not be thrilled to
discover that you left your IRA to your ex.

If your beneficiaries do not need the money (which, except
in the case of Roth plans, normally will be taxed as ordinary
income as it is withdrawn over ten years), you could name a
charity as the beneficiary of your retirement plan. Alternatively,
you could name the charity as a contingent beneficiary of an IRA
and let your heirs decide whether they want the IRA money or
not based on their financial circumstances at the time.

One possible advantage of leaving your retirement plan
to charity over deploying QCDs while you are alive is that all
the money can go to your family foundation or donor-advised
fund with no percentage-of-income limits on the amount. This
strategy can be advantageous for wealthy families facing the
40% estate tax.

You donate your IRA to charity by naming the charity on
your plan provider's beneficiary form. The rules governing

distributions to IRA beneficiaries are exasperating, and the penalties are exorbitant. Let's have a candid discussion about the issues involved.

Call your IRA custodian to find out their procedures for transferring IRAs to "entity" beneficiaries like a charity. What you want to hear is that they allow charities a one-time opportunity to withdraw the funds by submitting a piece of paper. What you don't want to hear is that the charity will have to open a beneficiary IRA to receive the payout. Why not?

As IRA guru Natalie Choate points out, "let's say that My Favorite University is governed by a board of 48 trustees; the IRA provider wants full information about each and every one of them--name, address, Social Security number, proof of citizenship, even information about each trustee's spouse, relatives, and business connections! ("Required by anti-money-laundering laws," says the IRA provider.)" Or, "it turns out that the entire staff of My Local Church is one elderly, overworked clergyman who has no time for complex paperwork."

You could also call the charity to inquire about their experience (if any) of receiving inherited IRAs from your custodian. If this is a big charity with a budget the size of a third-world country, they will be prepared for anything.

A donor-advised fund run by the same custodian as the IRA might be your best bet to serve as an intermediary between the donor and the end charity. You would have to consult with the DAF sponsor to see if this could be set up in a way that locks in your designated charities, or perhaps you could trust your heirs to honor your intentions. If this doesn't work, call some other custodians to see if they have policies in place to streamline this process and transfer your IRA to them.

What if you want to divide your IRA between, say, your children and a favorite charity?

For years, IRA rules made this a perilous decision. The risk was that combining a "nondesignated beneficiary," such as charity, alongside a "designated beneficiary," such as a human being, would force the IRA to dispense all the money to everyone on the short timetable of the "nondesignated beneficiary": five years. Taxwise, this is even more damaging than forcing all the money out over ten years, per the SECURE Act rules, and a must to avoid. The solution was to open a separate IRA for the charity alone and never mix beneficiary types.

Today, you can mix these two types of beneficiaries for a single IRA with a percentage allotted to each, provided that the executor of the estate divides the IRA into distinct inherited

IRAs by December 31 of the year following the death of the IRA owner. Verify this with a phone call to your custodian before commingling different categories of beneficiaries like humans and institutions, since changing the IRA rules seems to be a favorite hobby of Congress. Even the IRS has difficulty untangling these laws.

It is also okay to leave human beings as the primary beneficiaries and to name a charity as a contingent beneficiary in case any of the humans do not need or want the money. As before, call the IRA custodian to make sure the charity will get the money with a minimum amount of aggravation.

Consider that an IRA left to a family donor-advised fund or family foundation can occasionally substitute dollar-for-dollar for ordinary income. Perhaps your children will attend a church or synagogue, or they will serve on the board of a nonprofit, or their children will attend private schools, or their boss is involved with a charity. In such cases, your offspring might find it prudent to make contributions to these causes. Absent a family charitable vehicle, the children will have to dig into their own pockets and use after-tax dollars, making this an expensive form of charity. As we will see later, younger family members (including those in their forties or fifties) are usually not as well positioned to give to charity tax-efficiently as the senior members. Other things equal, it will save money for the family overall if charitable donations are funded by those who can do so at the least cost after-tax. If the younger adults have access to a family donor-advised fund that you handed down, they can give without having to touch their personal savings. This is a covert way of helping to build family wealth. It is also money less likely to be lost along the way through the customary divorce/drugs/dissipation process.

A word about Health Savings Accounts (HSAs). Unless inherited by a spouse, anyone else who receives them will have to pay taxes on the entire HSA balance that year at ordinary income rates, likely kicking them into a higher tax bracket in the process. All of the taxes; none of the benefits. HSAs are prime candidates to leave to charity.

We aren't done yet: there are specialized charitable uses for your IRA covered in the next two chapters.

# Chapter Seven

# Charitable **Trusts**

*"If you think tax is easy, you either don't understand the problem or you don't understand the solution."*

– Justin Miller

The legal structures we will talk about in this chapter are expensive, complicated, and customized to your exact circumstances. They are useful to a limited number of people. For instance:

- Rich people looking down the barrel of the 40% federal estate tax (i.e., those who have estates larger than 2025's $27.98 million Married/$13.99 million Single estate tax exemption)
- People who could use a large charitable deduction from their income tax this year due to a major one-time boost

in income—who also look forward to being in a lower tax bracket later and could benefit from deferring the income

- Affluent people who, while not facing the federal estate tax, nevertheless have million-dollar-plus retirement plans and high-bracket adult children who would prefer to stretch the beneficiary payouts over decades instead of pulling all the money out over ten years per the SECURE Act's tax-intensive timetable
- A family that wants to sell their low-basis family business but avoid paying capital gains taxes

If you are not one of these folks, there should be no great harm – and possibly some benefit – in skipping this chapter.

The legal structures that enable the split gifts are *irrevocable trusts*. There are two major kinds:

- The *charitable lead trust (CLT)*: You fund a trust, and the trust makes payouts to a charity for a designated term, and then whatever is left gets distributed to your family.
- The *charitable remainder trust (CRT)*: the payouts go to your family for a specified number of years, and then the remainder goes to charity.

Charitable Lead Trusts and Charitable Remainder Trusts are not the simplest way to give to charity. If your only goal were to support a charitable cause, it usually will be much easier and cheaper to donate directly.

Instead, these trusts benefit both the charity and the donor's family. In practice, these trusts also benefit the Brahmin class of high-priced professionals who assemble and administer them along with the end charities and the families.

While this is partially self-interested giving, it does benefit charities, and often very significantly. Will it be a "win-win" for both parties? You have to drill down into the details to see. As my friend Ben Stein puts it, it is not a question of "how" but of "how many."

It also depends on how the family defines winning. The ultimate win is to have more money via the trust than the family would have by inheriting the money directly. In this case, the gift to charity is the price the family pays for the tax benefits that let them leave more to their heirs. But this outcome is difficult to obtain.

Far more likely, the family will end up with a combination of money going to charity and the family, with less to family than they would have otherwise received but with more to charity than if they had made separate gifts to family and charity at the outset. It also assumes that the realized investment returns approximate long-term historical averages and that the set-up and operating costs of the trusts are manageable. Which is to say, in most cases, these trusts will require a charitable motivation on the part of the family.

We will not cover all the variations of these trusts but go straight to some basic examples of the most common types. If these look promising, your attorneys and financial advisors can point to any trust variants that might work better.

# The IRS 7520 Rate

The 7520 rate is an interest rate set monthly by the IRS and published online. Among other things, it is used to calculate both the present and remainder values of charitable trust annuities for tax purposes.

For Charitable Lead Trusts, it establishes the gift transfer taxes and the charitable deductions. For Charitable Remainder Trusts, it determines the minimum 10% charitable remainder and trust exhaustion rate, which also determines the minimum age for human annuity recipients.

Donors can choose from the three most recent monthly 7520 rates (and possibly a fourth month if they begin the trust near the start of a month).

Charitable Lead Trusts Perform better with low 7520 rates. These lower the payout to charity while setting an easier hurdle for the trust investments to outperform.

Charitable Remainder Trusts, on the other hand, benefit from higher 7520 rates. More money will be paid out to the family beneficiaries along the way, as the higher discount rate means less money needs to be set aside to fund the remainder going to charity.

## Charitable Lead Annuity Trusts

Here are the characteristics of the Charitable Lead Annuity Trusts (CLATs) we are going to consider in the cases below:

- An initial contribution of $1 million
- The CLAT is funded with nonappreciated assets, since they will forfeit any step up in basis that otherwise they might receive if they were included inside the donor's estate
- A long-term solution. The assets will be tied up in the CLAT for 10 to 30 years; the longer, the better
- The CLAT is invested in an S&P 500 Index fund and earns 7.37% a year (the average after-tax return of this fund since 2001)
- A "zeroed-out" tax structure where the payouts to charity exactly offset the taxes owed on the remainder

- A low IRS 7520 rate prevailing at the time the CLAT is created
- A family donor-advised fund (or possibly a family foundation) named as the charity beneficiary, preferably custodied at the same custodian as the trust assets
- A payout where the interest rate increases by 20% per year, maximizing the long-term compounding of principal inside the CLAT
- State income taxes are ignored

## Case 1 – A Testamentary CLAT vs. Estate Taxes

*Purpose:* To reduce estate taxes for a family with a large estate who has already used up their estate tax exemption.

How it works:

- The donor's estate creates a CLAT that pays a fixed amount to charity (the "annuity") each year for a set term
- After the term ends, the remaining assets go to the donor's children
- The CLAT is excluded from the donor's estate, reducing their estate taxes

Key points:

- Assets donated to the CLAT continue to grow

- The CLAT pays all the taxes on its income and gains
- The trust is designed so the annual payouts to charity per-fectly offset the gift taxes (40% of the value of the CLAT) owed on the money going to the kids

The trust's success depends on:

- Outperforming the IRS 7520 interest rate in force at the outset
- Investment returns that cover the trust taxes and expenses as well as the payouts
- Operating for a long time to allow assets to grow
- If investments underperform, the trust may run out of money before fulfilling its obligations

Example:

A wealthy family has used up all their exemptions and still sees the estate tax heading toward it like an asteroid from space. The aged head of the family decides to leave $1 million to a CLAT via his estate. It will be funded with an S&P 500 index fund that will receive a step up in cost basis and so contains no embedded capital gains.

Results:

Table 7.1 displays what is left over for heirs for the $1 million CLAT under different scenarios:

1. Three different applicable IRS 7520 interest rates at formation: 5%, 3%, and 1%

2. Three different CLAT terms: 10, 20 and 30 years

| | | Term | | |
|---|---|---|---|---|
| **TABLE 7.1: CLAT to Family & Charity** | | | | |
| **7520 Rate** | **$** | **10 years** | **20 years** | **30 years** |
| **5%** | To Heirs | $274,397 | $1,126,927 | $3,400,650 |
| | To Charity | $1,870,752 | $3,186,989 | $5,305,446 |
| **3%** | To Heirs | $485,773 | $1,870,994 | $5,259,408 |
| | To Charity | $1,646,427 | $2,401,566 | $3,349,641 |
| **1%** | To Heirs | $678,820 | $2,455,407 | $6,476,064 |
| | To Charity | $1,411,329 | $1,784,753 | $2,069,462 |
| **No CLAT: Pay Taxes and Invest Proceeds** | | | | |
| | To Heirs | $1,221,746 | $2,487,770 | $5,065,704 |
| | To Charity | $0 | $0 | $0 |

What stands out:

The lower the 7520 rate and the longer the duration of the trust, the better it works out for the heirs. While the charity also benefits from the long duration, it is hurt (just as the heirs are benefited) by a low 7520 rate (which sets the interest that is paid to charity).

The next thing to notice is that in all but two cases—both of them taking 30 years to establish—the heirs are better off in the "No CLAT" scenario: paying the 40% estate taxes on the million dollars and investing the after-tax money in the same S&P 500 index fund. It is not a win-win for the family in that sense. In a low-interest-rate environment (1%–3%) and after waiting for 30 years, the CLAT leaves them with more money than if they had inherited and invested with proceeds, but 30 years is a long time for children to wait for their marshmallow.

The story doesn't end there.

The CLAT gives them a larger pie. How much is the family paying for the charitable dollars that have been fed into and grown inside their donor-advised fund? Take the middle case: a 3% 7520 rate and a CLAT that runs for 20 years. We can calculate from Table 7.1 that the CLAT cost the family $616,776 in foregone returns relative to what they would have had if they had paid the estate taxes and invested the proceeds in a brokerage account over the same period. With the CLAT, the family would also have $2,401,566 untouched in their donor-advised fund available for charitable giving. That means they paid 26 cents ($616,776/$2,401,566) per dollar, which is a great deal for a charitably motivated family.

These numbers may not reflect the actual getting and spending along the way. For example, the lead annuity going to the donor-advised fund would be available for immediate distribution and might never compound to reach the dollar figures in Table 7.1. The remainder going to the family heirs would be a lump-sum distribution when the term of the trust ended, but in the alternative case where the family did not use a CLAT, paid the estate taxes, and reinvested the money left over, that money, too, would be available for immediate spending and so might never grow to the level forecast.

Could the result for the family be improved further? Perhaps, if the donor had started the clock on the CLAT during their lifetime, removing the assets from the estate (including its subsequent growth during the donor's lifetime). Also, if the family had committed more money to the CLAT, the final payout to the heirs would be proportionally higher.

## Case 2 - CLAT for an Income Tax Deduction

*Purpose:* To reduce taxes for a year with a one-time spike in income (e.g., from selling employee stock options, winning a case, or a big bonus).

How it works:

- Set up a zeroed-out "grantor" CLAT for the year of high income
- CLAT pays an annuity for a fixed term to a Donor-Advised Fund
- The grantor gets an immediate tax deduction for the future charitable donations
- After the CLAT's term ends, the grantor receives the remaining assets back tax-free

Key points:

- The discounted present value of the contribution to charity is pulled back to year one, even though the donations will be made over the life of the CLAT
- Both CLAT and Donor-Advised Fund are invested in an S&P 500 Index Fund
- The grantor pays the taxes on the interest, dividend, and capital gain income from the trust
- Donation limit: 30% of adjusted gross income
- Assumes an IRS 7520 rate of 3% and a term of 20 years
- A grantor CLAT is cheaper to run than a nongrantor CLAT since the taxes flow through to the grantor's tax return and the CLAT will not require an annual separate tax filing at higher trust tax rates

Example:

A 45-year-old Silicon Valley employee receives $1 million from the exercise of stock options in their startup. As grantor, they put the money into a zeroed-out, 20-year CLAT, investing it in an S&P 500 Index fund. In 20 years, the grantor/donor foresees being 65 and entering retirement, when their taxes will be much lower.

This strategy saves $370,000 (37% tax bracket x $1,000,000) on their income tax the first year.

Results:

After 20 years, CLAT terminates, and the Grantor receives $1.8 million, and their donor-advised fund has received $2.4 million.

| TABLE 7.2: $1,000,000 CLAT vs. Income Taxes | | |
|---|---|---|
| | CLAT | No CLAT |
| Term (years) | 20 | 20 |
| Income Tax Saving | $370,000 | $0 |
| Remainder | $1,870,992 | $2,612,159 |
| Donor-Advised Fund | $2,401,566 | $0 |

However, the employee would net more money by paying all the income taxes immediately and investing the proceeds for 20 years. This is not a win-win for both the donor and the charity if winning is defined as the donor coming out ahead personally in total dollars vs. not using a CLAT, regardless of the charitable contribution. Even a lower 7520 rate of 1% does not fix this problem. It requires some combination of a very low 7520 rate plus a longer term for the Grantor CLAT strategy for a purely self-interested donor to win.

On the other hand, the charitably motivated donor has, in effect, bought 2.4 million charity dollars for the difference between what they could have made without the CLAT and what they make using the CLAT, or $741,167, paying about thirty-one cents for each one. That is an excellent deal for a charity donor. If they didn't want to grow that big of a charity fund, they could always deal with this problem by setting up a smaller CLAT at the beginning.

Technical notes on CLATs:

These figures shown above do not include the expense of setting up the CLAT and administering it over decades. What would this cost? Perhaps $5,000+ a year, and more if the wealth management department of a private bank is running the show.

A family member serving as Trustee might draw a (taxable) 0.5% annual fee from a CLAT without raising any eyebrows, although the original donor could not do this.

The payouts due to charity and the gift taxes due on the remainder are both based on the monthly IRS 7520 interest rate in effect when the trust is created. The money left in the CLAT at termination goes to noncharity beneficiaries, such as the grantor or heirs. While the CLAT pays the gift tax on the *expected* value of the gift to the heirs calculated at the beginning, the *actual* value of the gift they receive in the end will depend on the investment returns over the CLAT's lifetime.

A CLAT is *not* a charity. The CLAT (at least a "nongrantor CLAT") is a taxpaying entity and will pay taxes on the income, dividends, and capital gains it generates every year. Assets placed inside a CLAT will be subject to capital gains taxes when sold.

A CLAT can hold discounted shares in a family LP or nonvoting shares of a family LLC or C corporation shares.

The beginning payouts to charity are quite low, but in our illustrations, these are stepped up every year by 20% for the duration of the CLAT. This strategy creates larger payouts to the end beneficiaries since more money compounds inside the CLAT for longer. In Private Letter Ruling 2012-16045, the IRS allowed a testamentary CLAT to increase its payout by 20% a year. There is nothing to stop you from setting up a "sharkfin" CLAT where the payouts are staged even more steeply, except that the IRS might disallow it and then where would you be?

One more risk: if the donor dies while a grantor CLAT is still in operation, there will be a partial income recapture to offset the initial charitable tax deduction the owner received.

# Charitable Remainder Unitrusts

A Charitable Remainder Unitrust (CRUT) is a type of charitable trust that:

- Provides income to beneficiaries (usually the donor or heirs) for either a set number of years or their lifetimes
- Donates the remaining assets to charity when the trust ends
- Offers tax benefits, including avoiding capital gains taxes on appreciated assets

Key points:

- Unlike the CLAT, the CRUT is a tax-exempt entity
- CRUTs can sell businesses or other appreciated assets tax-free
- They can potentially replace stretch IRAs and distribute inherited retirement accounts over the beneficiaries' lifetimes
- The trust must pay out at least 5% of its value annually to beneficiaries

- At least 10% of the initial value (determined by the IRS 7520 rate) must be projected to go to charity, which can be a donor-advised fund, family foundation, or other charity
- Complex rules govern beneficiary ages, payout rates, and trust administration
- When funded with IRAs, the donor's age at death affects how quickly assets must be moved into the CRUT
- Professional help is needed to set up and manage a CRUT properly
- Whether a CRUT is financially advantageous to the family will depend on many factors

When the "SECURE" Act eliminated the stretch IRA in 2019, your author proposed in the *Wall Street Journal* that a CRUT could restore the stretch. The stretch IRA had been foundational to estate planning for decades because it allowed children to inherit an IRA and then take the tax-deferred (or tax-free, in the case of a Roth IRA) withdrawals over their expected lifespans. Then, with a stroke of the pen, Congress killed it.

The SECURE Act was a coup by the insurance and financial services industry, which had lobbied to sell high-priced annuities inside our sacred IRA and 401(k) plans. The SECURE Act forced most nonspouse IRA beneficiaries to shoehorn their IRA withdrawals into a ten-year window, with these supersized withdrawals typically hitting beneficiaries in their high-earning years. The result: more of your money grabbed by the government, less passed on to your family.

IRS Private Letter Ruling #1990-1023 established that you can leave your IRA as an irrevocable gift to a charitable trust. As we have mentioned, Traditional IRAs are among the worst assets for a beneficiary to inherit since all the distributions are taxed as ordinary income. Only one IRA can be used to fund a CRUT; if both marital partners want to leave their IRAs to CRUTs, each must fund separate trusts.

## Case 1 – A CRUT horse race against an IRA

We compare leaving a $1 million IRA to a CRUT for a 35-year-old daughter, while another $1 million IRA is left directly to her brother. Both are invested in the S&P 500.

Initial Advantage: The money destined for the CRUT can grow tax-free for five years inside the IRA before funding the CRUT, while the IRA distributions going directly to the heir must begin the following year.

Results without fees:

- CRUT: Daughter receives $22.7 million over her 45-year remaining lifetime, with $2.8 million left to charity
- Direct IRA: Brother gets $19.5 million over 45 years

Results with 1% CRUT management fee:

- CRUT: Daughter receives $18.8 million
- Direct IRA: Brother still receives $19.5 million

Key points:

- CRUT takes 34 years to surpass inheriting the IRA
- Long-term compounding can benefit both heirs and charity
- CRUT effectiveness is highly dependent on expenses

Recommendations:

- Use major custodians for seamless transitions from IRA to CRUT to Charity
- Carefully vet all details with the account custodian
- Consider the heir's circumstances (age, tax bracket, financial stability)

Narrative:

The case illustrates that while CRUTs can potentially provide more value, their effectiveness depends on factors like management costs and time horizon.

The IRA balance of $1 million is left to a testamentary CRUT. Because the donor died more than five years before his RMD started, his executor wisely took five years to transfer the money into the CRUT, during which time it has appreciated tax-free at 7.7%/year in an S&P 500 Index fund. The 7520 rate is a favorable 5%—yes, in the upside-down world of CRUTs (unlike with the CLATs), the HIGHER the 7520 rate, the better for the human heirs.

Part of what makes the CRUT attractive is the set of assumptions built into the applicable 2010 IRS longevity tables. People have been living slightly longer than these tables estimate—especially the affluent, salad-eating types who are likely to be named as CRUT beneficiaries. The table's front-end charitable deduction might be pegged too high. The CRUT table projects the beneficiary will die young, leaving more of the trust to charity.

Here, the donor has left the CRUT to his 35-year-old daughter, who has a life expectancy of 45 years. She takes the maximum allowable distribution every year—6.05%—that will leave the minimum 10% of the CRUT to charity.

However, her father had a love child. He secretly arranged for this child—her brother—to inherit a million-dollar IRA, but with no CRUT structure. This IRA is transferred to the heir over ten years, following the applicable IRS distribution rules. Both children pay taxes at the top Federal rates, and both invest in the same S&P 500 index fund, which they let compound and never touch.

Who wins?

| TABLE 7.3: $1,000,000 CRUT vs. IRA | | |
|---|---|---|
| | CRUT | IRA |
| Charitable Deduction | $134,820 | $0 |
| Final Amount to Charity | $2,827,920 | $0 |
| CRUT Management Fee | 0% | N/A |
| $ to Beneficiary | $22,706,519 | $19,539,847 |

By this reckoning, the daughter wins. On her deathbed, she has over $22 million in her brokerage account, plus the CRUT will make a big donation to her donor-advised fund for her children to dole out. Her brother has only $19 million and will have nothing for charity either.

And yet. . .

Things are not quite as great as they appear. For the first thirty-four years, the son had more money. That's how long it took for the CRUT to catch up.

Also, there is something dreamy and unrealistic about the daughter's situation. Both she and her brother paid the 0.03% annual management fee and 0.34% taxes for the mutual fund. But what about that 0% fee to establish and maintain the CRUT? Someone had to draft the CRUT documents, serve as trustee, do the investing, accounting, and tax preparation, and so on. I can easily imagine a bank charging 1% for this service.

Now things don't look so pretty.

| TABLE 7.4: $1,000,000 CRUT vs. IRA | | |
|---|---|---|
| | CRUT | IRA |
| Charitable Deduction | $134,820 | $0 |
| Final Amount to Charity | $1,556,539 | $0 |
| CRUT Management Fee | 1% | N/A |
| $ to Beneficiary | $18,818,184 | $19,539,934 |

After forty-five years, the daughter lies on her deathbed filled with anger and regret, all because her brother got more money than she did. Had she been more charitably minded, she might have taken comfort in having bought 1.5 million charity dollars for the difference between what her brother got and what she did, or $721,750. She effectively paid 43 cents for each charity dollar.

If the payout stretches long enough, and the CRUT is invested aggressively, the beneficiaries can come out ahead in absolute terms. But this is not the common result.

These projections may never come true. The most egregious assumption is that the brother and sister would sit watching their respective accounts accumulate for forty-five years without spending a nickel. Many of those dollars probably would be spent immediately. Only the payout to the family donor-advised fund is safe because it will arrive in a lump sum after the brother and sister have passed away.

Your custodian needs to be on board with the whole plan. I would use Fidelity, Schwab, or Vanguard since they could hold the IRA, then the Trust, and finally the family donor-advised fund, all in-house for a seamless transition. Do not underestimate the catastrophic problems that might arise with these handoffs from entity to entity in the event you don't have these ducks in a row. Have the relevant departments at your custodian review the trust documents to make sure everything is copacetic. Then check back with them every so often to make sure their policies have not changed, jeopardizing your estate plan.

# An IRA-to-CRUT Checklist

- You should not have a taxable estate
- Your heirs should be in a high tax bracket
- Heirs should be young but not too young to qualify under the unknown but possibly low 7520 rates applicable when the CRUT is finally created
- Heirs should be insurable so they can buy term-life policies to make their beneficiaries whole in the event they die young
- Heirs should be financially comfortable waiting for the money and receiving it in variable annual payouts instead of being given immediate access to the large lump sum of their dreams
- Bonus points: Heirs are legally or financially sophisticated enough to administer and invest the trust themselves, so the CRUT is not ravaged by high overhead expenses

You won't know how this works out for decades, by which time you and everyone who set this up for you will be unavailable for comment except via Ouija board.

## Case 2 – The CRUT sells a closely held business

Scenario: A family wants to sell their zero-cost-basis business, now worth $1 million.

Options:

- Sell directly, paying $238,000 in federal capital gains taxes, or
- Use a Charitable Remainder Trust, avoiding capital gains taxes

CRUT Setup:

- Two beneficiaries, ages 35 and 45, resulting in a 52-year estimated payout
- Invested in Vanguard Total Stock Market index fund and taking a 5.1% annual distribution to heirs
- No administrative or management fees
- 7520 Rate is 5%

Results:

- CRUT: $24,765,698 to beneficiaries, $3,919,213 to charity, or
- Direct sale of business (paying taxes and investing): $26,219,754 to beneficiaries

Key points:

- In this example, the CRUT never outperforms a direct sale
- The charitable deduction is limited to 20-30% of AGI, depending on the type of charity beneficiary
- Early death of an heir is a risk; life insurance could mitigate at a price
- Any CRUT management fees further reduce the CRUT payout to heirs

Considerations:

- Qualified appraisal needed for the business
- Discount applied to tax deduction due to lack of marketability and control
- CRUT must be established and funded before there is a binding sale agreement

Narrative:

The case demonstrates that a CRUT can potentially provide financial benefits when selling a highly appreciated asset. Still, the advantages depend on factors like low management fees and a long holding period.

The family wants to sell the family business, but it has a zero-cost basis and today is worth $1 million. That's $238,000 straight to the Feds in capital gains taxes (not counting state taxes) triggered by the sale.

On the other hand, they could put the company into a Charitable Remainder Trust. Assuming the family can thread the needle described in the earlier chapter on Donating Securities, the business can be sold with no capital gains taxes with all the proceeds reinvested for income. The company would need a qualified appraisal, and the determination of fair market value would include a discount for lack of marketability and control (we assumed 20%). The business must be contributed to the CRUT before there is a binding sale agreement in place.

There are two beneficiaries, ages 35 and 45. The last survivor has 48 years projected for the income to compound inside the CRUT. They invest the money in the Vanguard Total Stock Market index fund, which has a compound return since 2001 of 7.99% pretax and 7.65% after-tax. The family can take a tax deduction on the present value of the estimated final gift to charity. This deduction is limited to 20% of their adjusted gross income if the charity is a private foundation and 30% of AGI if it is a public charity. The family also set aside the tax savings of $80,000 ($1 million FMV—20% discount for lack of liquidity and control x 10% for CRUT residual payout to charity) from donating the business to the CRUT, invested it in the Total Stock Market fund, and then gave it to the kids, who added it to their savings and let it continue to grow.

| TABLE 7.5: $1,000,000 CRUT vs. Sale | | |
|---|---|---|
| | CRUT | No CRUT |
| Charitable Deduction | $80,000 | $0 |
| Final DAF Balance | $3,919,213 | $0 |
| CRUT Management Fee | 0% | N/A |
| $ Beneficiaries' Balance | $24,765,698 | $26,219,754 |

With the CRUT, the family sells the business for $1 million, pays no taxes, invests the proceeds in the index fund, and takes the maximum 5.1% distribution out every year for the heirs, who pay capital gains taxes on it at 23.8% and then deposit it in the same index fund, this time inside their brokerage account.

In the alternative case, the family sells the business, pays the 23.8% capital gains taxes, and also invests it in the index fund. This approach wins right out of the gate, and the CRUT never catches up.

With such a long payout interval, the possibility of one heir prematurely dying is nontrivial. Term life insurance for all heirs would address this—provided they are all insurable—but that is another cost.

Unfortunately, this presentation was for a zero-expense option. A 0.5% fee for annual CRUT expenses is a further dead-weight drag on the CRUT's performance.

Is it worth keeping a CRUT running for half a century for your descendants to have the extra $3.9 million in the donor-advised fund? In effect, they have sacrificed $1.4 million in returns to get the $3.9 million, paying 37 cents for each dollar of charity. In practice, it is unlikely the heirs would have let their annuity compound in their taxable account until their death before touching it.

There are other important types of CRUTs, such as the NIMCRUT and the FLIP NIMCRUT. If the CRUT idea might work for you, discuss it with your attorney and let them lay out the options.

More Technical Notes on CRUTs:

The CRUT is a "nondesignated" beneficiary of an IRA, leading to some surreal but important consequences.

If the donor dies more than five years before they were scheduled to begin taking RMDs, his trustee has five years to empty the IRA into the CRUT, starting January 1 of the year after the donor's death. To optimize this, he should make no distributions during years 1-4 and then move all the money over to the CRUT at the end of year 5. The CRUT is established as of the date of death, but with no money to pay out, no distributions can be made.

On the other hand, if the donor dies after having already begun taking RMDs, a different set of rules applies. While the trustee has the option to transfer the IRA assets into the CRUT at any time, the trustee should let the corpus continue to grow tax-deferred inside the IRA for as long as possible. This means using what is called the donor's "ghost life expectancy," moving the money over every year in scheduled RMD-sized amounts until the donor's actuarially predicted date of death. Spooky, but it should be financially beneficial to the family, provided the beneficiaries are willing to wait for it.

The CRUT's 10%-to-charity is only an estimate. In practice, the charity will get whatever is left after the last CRUT beneficiary dies. It doesn't matter to the IRS if the amount is less than the 10% initially promised, provided all the rules have been followed. This gives the end charity a stake in the CRUT being invested and administered properly.

You will want to use financial software (such as Estate View, Tiger Tables, or Number Cruncher) to discover the highest allowable distribution rate for your heirs. The free CRUT calculators I have seen online are marketing toys, and I cannot recommend them. If you are serious, pay your accountant, financial planner, or estate attorney to run the numbers for you.

The CRUT is an income tax strategy, not an estate tax strategy. In the face of estate taxes, it will be more advantageous to leave the IRA to heirs directly so they can take a deduction for the estate tax against their inherited IRA income. A CRUT beneficiary gets no credit for this until all other types of income have been withdrawn. By that time, the estate tax deduction probably will have been forgotten or lost over the decades (as well as cut in half by inflation).

Key points about Charitable Remainder Unitrust (CRUT) distributions:

Distribution Order: CRUT distributions follow a strict "worst-out first" order:

Tier 1: Ordinary income

Tier 2: Capital gains

Tier 3: Tax-free income

Tier 4: Return of principal

Complex Administration: Managing a CRUT requires meticulous tracking and accounting of all income types, which can be challenging and expensive.

Initial Distributions: For CRUTs funded by IRAs, initial distributions are taxed as ordinary income, typically for 15-20 years.

While CRUT proponents sometimes advocate letting the family-member trustees handle everything—investing, administration, taxes—these responsibilities are nontrivial and highly consequential. Every dollar that comes into the CRUT needs to be tracked until it leaves, segregated by the type of trust accounting income it represents. The trustee keeps a running annual total of each type and makes distributions down the tiers, prorated within the income classes subject to the same tax rate in each tier.

Brokerage statements are not segregated into these categories, much less with a historical running total of each. Who is going to figure this out and meticulously track it over the decades, cutting the checks, preparing K-1s for beneficiaries, and filing tax returns with the IRS? Your son-in-law, the surfer? Have him check out IRS Form 5227 and the twenty pages of gnarly instructions that accompany it. In other words, there are going to be meaningful annual expenses to oversee this safari after you have peeled off for the Endless Summer.

If an IRA funded the CRUT, it is entirely pretax and goes to your beneficiaries as ordinary income (just as the IRA would have done). Working through this part will probably take fifteen to twenty years.

Two states—Pennsylvania and New Jersey—do not recognize CRUTs as tax-exempt. They want to tax income as it accrues inside the CRUT and expect your CRUT to file a state tax return. Check with your tax advisors to see if there are any workarounds.

Instead of pulling the money out of the CRUT based on the life expectancy of the beneficiaries, you have the option of letting the CRUT run for a fixed term. But the longest that term can run is twenty years (twenty-five years if we count an extra five years to move the money from your IRA to the CRUT). It is not easy to get your money back over that short of a time.

## Final Thoughts on Charitable Trusts and Split Gifts

Set these up carefully, in full consultation with your estate attorney, accountant, financial advisor, and custodian. Each of the professionals has their own angles to consider. While it will be cheaper for you to work with a charity offering an off-the-shelf product, this stacks the split gifts in the charity's favor, and there will be no backing out if you change your mind about the charity. This flexibility is why a family DAF makes a great charity beneficiary.

In practice, the "annuity" portion on the trust is distributed first, and so available to be spent along the way—either on charity (with a CLAT) or on personal consumption (with a CRUT). The remainder at the end of the trust's term will be whatever the market gods deliver, but will arrive in a lump sum to the heirs (or more likely the heirs' beneficiaries, since their deaths have triggered the end of the CLAT) or as a lump sum to the DAF (presumably to be used by the heirs' beneficiaries).

To accomplish your goals, pay for a customized solution. The trusts are irrevocable, which means what it says. These might cost $5,000–$10,000 to set up and possibly much more if you have large, complicated holdings. Administrative, investment, and accounting fees are on top of this. These fees need to be built into your proof-of-concept.

In all these scenarios, you must include:

- The all-in costs and benefits of the counterfactual situation where you do not use a trust
- A realistic inclusion of all fees for the establishment and maintenance of the trust over time, with legal, accounting, investment, and even insurance expenses (if any are contemplated) built into the model
- Explicit projections of future investment returns and tax rates, with the model run under varying scenarios and assumptions for a 360-degree look at possible outcomes

- A calculation of how much the charity dollars will cost you in underperformance relative to the option of not using the trust
- Weighing the likelihood that the distributions either to heirs or to a DAF will be spent immediately by heirs with other priorities than maximizing total returns on a spreadsheet.
- The same circumspection when viewing the no-trust counterfactual: will the beneficiaries sit around eating Cheerios while watching their investment accounts grow for decades, or will they spend the money as fast as it comes in?

The professionals across the desk from you are probably top-rank. You will have to take a deep dive into the details. These trusts can work well, but go into them with eyes open.

# Chapter Eight

# Prepackaged Split Gifts **To Charity**

This chapter discusses annuities. If you are the type of person who would never buy an annuity, you can skip it.

### Charitable Gift Annuities

Many charities will happily offer you an income stream. You donate to a charity today, and then the charity pays you (or you and your spouse) a fixed annuity for the rest of your lives. When you die, the charity gets whatever is left.

The charity's finances are backing the annuity, so you need to evaluate its probable solvency over the coming decades.

Since the charity can sell any property you donate without paying taxes, in theory, it has more cash to put toward the annuity than you would if you were to sell the property and pay the capital gains taxes, leaving only the after-tax dollars to annuitize. With the charity gift annuity, you still have to pay the capital gains taxes, but these are spread out over your life expectancy as part of each check you receive. You also get an immediate tax deduction for the present value of the end amount projected to go to charity.

If the annuity was funded with appreciated stocks, the annuity comes back to you as a mixture of capital gains and tax-free return of principal, in exactly the proportion as they stood when you made the original donation. If you live long enough, the character of the annuity payout will eventually turn into 100% ordinary income.

If you are looking for an annuity for both you and your spouse, it might be better first to give the appreciated asset that will fund the annuity to the younger spouse (using the unlimited marital deduction) and then base the annuity payout on the younger spouse's expected lifespan. That way, the annuity's tax bill will be spread over a longer duration. The charity might also be willing to write a deferred annuity to take effect when you retire years from now. A deferred annuity would require even greater faith in the charity's longevity and solvency, not to mention its long-term effectiveness and fidelity to its mission. These are not small matters.

Annuities have the potentially catastrophic downside of offering no inflation protection. Buying one demonstrates your faith in the government's ability to achieve and maintain price stability across decades. Curiously, no insurance carrier will sell a true CPI inflation-indexed annuity. Should that be telling us something? Some will let you pay more to buy an "annual step-up" for your payout of, say, 1% to 3% a year—but that is more like the *opposite* of inflation protection. If you are worried about inflation, you should want to be paid back as quickly as possible (and preferably not buy an annuity at all) instead of buying an even more expensive policy where you use more valuable dollars today to buy more low-value, inflated dollars tomorrow.

Annuities are irrevocable. You are getting married to the charity and the annuity, so you should love both. Over a retirement horizon, you can typically do better investing the money yourself, selling some of your assets every year to cover living expenses, and then leaving the remainder as a bequest to charity if that is your intent. Since this is your standard of living in retirement that is at stake, this latter approach has the advantage of letting the charity shoulder the risk, not you. Alternatively, if you can afford it, donate to the charity over your retirement through Qualified Charitable Distributions from your IRA.

# QCDs to Charitable Gift Annuities

SECURE Act 2.0 allowed you to make a one-time Qualified Charitable Distribution of up to $54,000 from your IRA to buy an annuity from a public charity. This counts toward the $108,000 QCD annual limit for 2025, but you only receive a tax benefit if the amount is also equal to or less than your required minimum distribution. It would be better for everyone if Congress would raise the $54,000 limit to match the $108,000 QCD limit.

Not every public charity will have this option, although the larger ones probably will. The minimum allowed payout for the QCD annuity is 5% annually and it must begin within one year. The American Council on Gift Annuities sets the rate in nearly all cases. They assume the charity will need 1% in operational expenses to run the annuity and will want to set aside half the amount originally contributed for itself. Some colleges may offer better deals than this (see Pomona College, for example) while also having higher credit scores than other charities and insurance companies. It would be prudent to check the credit rating of both the charity as well as any insurance company to which they subcontract the policy.

SECURE Act 2.0 also will let you move $54,000 one time from your IRA to a Charitable Remainder Unitrust or a Charitable Remainder Annuity Trust, but this amount is too small to work efficiently. The expense of creating this vehicle and administering it over the years might be greater than the cash flow to either you or the charity. Even the big charities that can put you in their off-the-shelf CLATs and CRUTs are looking for $108,000 as a minimum contribution, and their offerings will not usually advantage your side of the table.

The 2025 QCD to charitability annuity limit at least has the virtue of spreading out $54,000 of your required minimum distribution over the rest of your life instead of paying taxes on the whole sum this year.

The maximum $54,000 QCD cannot be commingled with other funds to buy a larger annuity, and your payout will consist entirely of ordinary income. These QCD charitable annuities must start within one year and can only extend through your life (or your and your spouse's lives).

Compare the charity's offer to the alternatives, such as buying a *Qualified Longevity Annuity Contract* (QLAC) directly inside your IRA using up to $200,000 pretax. Many insurance companies would be competing for your dollars here, and this allows you to make a larger purchase, but it has no benefit to charities.

# Testamentary Charitable Annuity

In a Testamentary Charitable Annuity, you make your charity the beneficiary of your IRA, and the charity promises to issue an annuity (which will be 100% ordinary income, just as if it came from an IRA) for your heirs. You negotiate the details while you are still alive. Your beneficiaries get the annuity, and the charity gets the remainder. However, an IRA left directly to your heirs should generate higher returns, especially if invested primarily in stocks.

A Charitable Annuity will typically go to a married couple, so first-to-die is not an issue. But for a Testamentary Charitable Annuity going to several kids or grandkids, whoever dies first loses. The purchase of term life insurance for all beneficiaries will reduce the payout further, tilting the scales toward leaving the IRA directly to heirs without the annuity detour.

As an investment advisor, whenever I see a dual-purpose product that someone wants to sell my clients, I assume there is some deliberate obfuscation going on. Bundled transactions are almost invariably problematic because, as we have seen, it is difficult to optimize for two conflicting outcomes: money for you vs. money for charity. A cleaner solution might be to leave a percentage of your IRA to your charity.

# Pooled Income Fund

This is a vehicle where you toss your appreciated assets into a pool for a prorated charitable deduction today. Then, the entire pool of investments is used to generate a quarterly pro-rated payout to all the donors (or other named lifetime income beneficiaries). This payout is not tax-advantaged—it is the usual sandwich of interest, dividends, and capital gains. It will vary from quarter to quarter with the performance of the pool as well as depending on the amount you originally donated and your life expectancy. The pool pays out all the income based on its previous three-year return history, which heavily favors the end charity during times of low interest rates.

There are also "new" pooled income funds, which have liberated themselves from this three-year history ("new" here means under three years old) and instead pay out the IRS 7520 rate (4.8% as of September 2025) minus 1%, for a net 3.8% payout. This return may not get your heart racing. They can pay a higher rate if they can earn it, which might make them more competitive.

The few I have looked at have not been a "win-win" for the donor or the charity, but rather a win for the pooled income fund sponsor due to the high fees. No surprises there—that is the business model of the financial services industry. But there may be some great ones I missed.

Since you have no control over the fund once you have jumped into the pool, make sure you examine it closely before investing. I do question whether people with high-performing investment portfolios would ever put them in a pooled income fund. I fear there might be some adverse selection bias at work.

# Chapter Nine

# Gifts of **Property**

If you do not contemplate donating tangible property to charity, do yourself a great favor and skip this chapter.

Let me tell you a secret: The IRS is not wild about your giving property to charity unless it is raw land or a building that can be readily sold or rented. Once you wander off this reservation, giving becomes much more complicated. If donating property is your game, study IRS Publication 526 on charitable contributions and IRS Publication 561 on property to learn what lies in store for you. These cover all the main categories: clothing, household items in good condition, cars, boats, airplanes, collectibles, real estate, life insurance, patents, licenses, etc. The further you stray from cash and stocks and bonds, and the larger the dollar amounts you claim, the more difficult the transaction is going to become. Proceed with caution.

Here is another secret: charities feel the same way. Most charities—unless this is their business model (e.g., Goodwill, a $6.1 billion business operating as a charity)—do not want your old junk. They prefer a check. Consider whether a charity's junk-accepting mission, if they offer one, is really a nuisance they use as a door-opener to collect what they really want: donors with checkbooks.

Our treatment will be brisk but will offer some idea of the playing field. The list here is potentially endless, and each subcategory of property might include only a small percentage of donors, so this will be a brief primer.

# Art

Artist Robert Ryman sold a canvas that he painted white for $15,000,000. If I paint a canvas white, can I donate it to charity and (conceding that his painting is better than mine) perhaps take a modest $1,000,000 deduction?

No. The IRS limits the deduction to my cost basis or to my painting's reasonable value, whichever is less. Perhaps five dollars?

Consider this scenario: in Paris fifty years ago, strolling the Champs Elysee with your main squeeze, you bought a Renoir sketch for $10,000. Now you take it on *Antiques Roadshow*, and their experts gush that it is worth $150,000. You decide to give it to your favorite charity, the American Heart Association. How much can you deduct?

Answer: $10,000, your cost basis. The reason is that the Renoir is not relevant to the charity's mission. Donate it to the Metropolitan Museum of Art instead. That way, you could deduct the painting's fair market value. But—don't break out the Dom Perignon yet. If your charity sells the donated art (and they must tell the IRS if they do within three years of receiving the donation), this is a big clue that it was not related to their mission and that your deduction probably should have been limited to your cost basis. In that case, expect a letter from the IRS soon. It won't be good news.

Could you show the IRS agent your starring segment on *Antiques Roadshow* in support of your deduction? No. Any gift or gifts of personal property alleged to be worth more than $5,000 requires a *qualified appraisal* from a *qualified appraiser*, noting that it is being prepared specifically for tax purposes.

The IRS closely scrutinizes art donations. As the IRS Commissioner warns, "Creativity in art is a beautiful thing, but aggressive creativity in art donation deductions can paint a bad picture for people pulled into these schemes."

## Gifts of Real Estate

The rules around donating real estate are so complicated and contingent on situation-specific particulars that even this book cannot guide you. Talk to your legal and tax professionals who have expertise in this area.

## Conservation Easements

These involve donating ownership rights to a piece of land to the government or a land trust in exchange for a charitable deduction of its fair market value. This sounds innocent enough, but then syndicators got involved in marketing shares in these transactions to rubes, exaggerating the valuations to claim grossly inflated tax deductions. These easements quickly rose through the ranks to become one of the IRS's "Top Twelve" tax scams.

Then, in an about-face, the IRS announced a generous settlement for their outstanding easement audits, offering to end their threat of 40% penalties if taxpayers would settle by paying a 21% tax and 5% penalty. Maybe the agency is feeling generous since its recent acquisition of $60 billion in fresh funding.

While the IRS has made a big deal about conservation easements, I'm not sure how big a problem this really is. I have been in conference rooms full of accountants where no one could recall ever having dealt with one.

## Collectibles

Collectibles can be great to donate (if you can find a charity willing to accept them) because they are taxed to you at 28% instead of 15% or 20% for other capital gain property. Surprisingly, precious metals are also taxed as collectibles: the exchange-traded fund for the SPDR Gold Shares (GLD) is backed by gold bars in a vault in London, but these still are considered "collectibles" and so taxed at 28% for capital gains (and 31.8% with the Net Investment Income Tax added). These could be a priority to donate when combing through your investment portfolio.

## Donating your time

You may earn $750/hour as an attorney in your day job, but as far as the IRS is concerned, your time driving nails at Habitat for Humanity is worth nothing. You are entitled to deduct transportation expenses driving to and from the charity job site, but if you earn $750/hour it may not be worth your time to claim 14 cents a mile, either.

Charities differ widely in their need for volunteers. In some cases, volunteers are an integral part of their service mission.

In others, they are a nuisance. Find out which yours is before showing up at their HQ.

# Insurance Policies

Since most insurance policies are paid tax-free to beneficiaries, these would seem a low-priority asset to donate to charity – but rest assured, it can be done.

A paid-up policy can be donated to charity with the charity additionally named as beneficiary. You must make the charity the owner of all economic rights to the policy.

The value of the gift is its fair market value, what a willing buyer and seller would agree upon. This value is usually interpolated by finding what the carrier would sell an equivalent policy for today (to the now older insured party), plus or minus any unearned premiums, dividends, and loans (and no debt is allowed on a policy donated to charity). A second way to calculate it is to take the sum of the premiums paid minus any withdrawals. The charitable deduction would be the lesser of these two calculations.

If the policy requires servicing with ongoing premiums, the donor can make the tax-deductible payments himself or donate cash to the charity and have them make the payments.

# Adjusted Gross Income Limits

Do AGI giving limits apply when donating property? You bet!

Table 9.1 summarizes the percentage of Adjusted Gross Income you can give to charities each year:

| TABLE 9.1: % of AGI Annual Deduction Limits | | | |
|---|---|---|---|
| | Cash and Property | Capital Gain Property | "Unrelated" C.G. Property |
| Type of Valuation | Fair Market Value | Fair Market Value | Cost Basis Only |
| **Public Charities** | 60% | 30%* | 20%** |
| **Private Foundations** | 30% | 20%*** | 20% |

\* Or 50% if limited to basis

\*\* Or Fair Market Value, if less

\*\*\* Only for publicly traded stock, not property

Capital Gain property is anything that can be sold for more than you paid for it. It could be stocks, real estate, art, a family business, etc. "Unrelated" Capital Gain Property (the third column on Table 9.1) is when the property is not used in the charity's mission, like the Renoir going to the American Heart Association in the previous example. These all must be long-term (held > 1 year) capital gains.

The tax code contains a stark prejudice: donating to a registered public charity offers a much better tax break than donating to your family foundation. Donors typically collect the full fair market value when they go to a public charity but are limited to the cost basis when they go to a private foundation—and that at a much lower percentage of their adjusted gross income. The exception would be a private *operating* foundation—one that is actively engaged in direct charitable work and follows all the rules to document this.

Most donors do not give to other people's private foundations. The giving requirements are restrictive, and they would surrender all control over how the money was used. A major exception is Warren Buffett, who made major donations of Berkshire Hathaway shares to the Bill & Melinda Gates Foundation. Even then, he served as a Trustee, with oversight into how the money would be invested and granted.

## Rules for Giving

Gifts of property below $250 need a record showing the name of the charity, its location, the date, the value, and the item's condition. A receipt from the charity would be pleasant. Charities such as Goodwill and the Salvation Army have guides right on their website to help you realistically value the property you donate. If you don't use these, the IRS may well wonder why not.

Imagine having to document your gift to an unsmiling IRS agent and proceed accordingly. This is a game of "The Price is Right" where you are on your honor setting the value. The more evidence you can offer, the better—remembering that someone who appears to be slippery or dishonest in one part of Form 1040 is more likely to be dishonest elsewhere and merit close examination.

Gifts of property over $250 but under $500 additionally require a written acceptance from the charity saying what you gave and whether you received anything of value in exchange. You still estimate the value.

Gifts of property totaling over $500 must be accompanied by a contemporaneous letter from the charity indicating the value and stating that you received nothing of value in return for your donation. At this level, you get to file Form 8283, Section A, which is the catch-all form for Noncash Charitable Contributions from $500 on up. You state the date you acquired the property, how you came to own it, and what you paid for it. All this adds color to your story. You also need to maintain these records. However enjoyable the process of donating property might have been up to this point, you will find that Form 8283 takes the fun out of it.

For gifts of property totaling over $5,000, you need to add a qualified appraisal from a qualified appraiser. You report this in Section B of Form 8283. The qualified appraiser signs off on the valuation in Part IV of Form 8283.

For gifts of art valued at $20,000 or more, the qualified appraisal must be thoroughly documented and attached to your return. For art valued at over $50,000, along with the qualified appraisal, you must request a Statement of Value directly from the IRS. It will cost you an additional nondeductible $7,500 for the IRS's gimlet-eyed experts to appraise up to three items for you.

The IRS enforces these rules to the letter. Be prepared.

In the 2022 case of Albrecht v. Commissioner, Martha Albrecht donated $463,676 worth of historic Indian artifacts to an Indian museum in Santa Fe. Because she failed to obtain the letter from the museum stating that she received nothing of value in return for this donation, the IRS disallowed the deduction, and the tax court agreed. No problem—she went back to the museum to collect a letter stating she had received nothing of value. The IRS rejected it, saying it was not *contemporaneous* with her gift, and the tax court concurred. After a tax return is filed, it is too late to go back and get the letter. Without the letter of acknowledgment in good form, you don't get the deduction, and you can't fix it later.

Any deduction of over $500,000 must include a qualified appraisal unless it is cash, inventory, publicly traded stock, or intellectual property. No qualified appraisal means no deduction.

When you donate cash, there is no question about value, and there is almost always a paper trail. But when you donate tangible property other than real estate, things become subjective very quickly. If you are claiming a high-dollar deduction, be concerned about the qualified appraisal from the qualified appraiser that you attach to your tax return along with Form 8283. There are a lot of rules and requirements, and the IRS will be quick to pounce on any mistakes.

The IRS attaches stiff penalties if you overestimate the value of your donated property and underpay your taxes as a result. The penalty tops out at 40% if the professed value turns out to be twice the determined value and your taxes were underpaid by more than $5,000 as a result. There are cases where someone filed their tax return claiming a large deduction, but instead of a deduction, they got a large fine with no opportunity to fix anything.

As an aside, the most famous case involving bad appraisals involved the estate of the white-gloved King of Pop,

Michael Jackson himself. Who got in trouble? This time, it was the IRS.

The agency made a huge strategic error. They picked one valuation expert to value three unrelated assets of the estate: Jackson's name and likeness, Jackson's interest in the Sony/ATV catalog (which included the Beatles' songs), and Jackson's own MIJAC music catalog.

Worse, the IRS's expert lied under oath, claiming he had never worked for the IRS before and that he had never written a valuation report for the IRS before. He told the court he did not advertise to promote business. Then Jackson's attorneys produced evidence where he claimed to be "the expert of the century" in a "billion-dollar tax case."

The judge was not pleased. He rejected the IRS expert's analysis as "fantasy" and agreed with Jackson's lawyers that he had "valued the wrong asset, included unforeseeable events in his valuation, and miscalculated the asset's value." The judge said the expert's testimony, "quite apart from the taint of the perjury, is unreliable and unpersuasive."

But I digress.

Here are a few pointers to help you build the record you need to navigate this minefield:

| TABLE 9.2: Documenting Deductions for Property ||
|---|---|
| **Category** | **Documentation, briefly...** |
| Property under $250 | Name of charity, location, date, the items, condition, value |
| Property $250 - $500 | Additionally requires a contemporaneous letter of acceptance from the charity saying what you gave, the date, the total amount, and attesting that you received nothing in return |
| Property > $500 | Additionally requires Form 8283, asking for more details about the property, such as when you bought it, from whom, and how much you paid |
| Property > $5,000 | Additionally requires Section B of Form 8283, including a summary of the qualified appraisal from a qualified appraiser |
| Art > $20,000 | Additionally requires the qualified appraisal to be attached to the tax return |
| Art > $50,000 | Additionally requires a Statement of Value directly from the IRS. |
| Property > $500,000 | The complete signed appraisal must be attached to the tax return along with Form 8283 |

What is in the appraisal engagement letter?

- Names the client (a person? A trust?) who will be donating the property and submitting the tax form to the IRS

- Names the specific property that will be donated and for which the appraisal is sought

- Indicates whether the communications among the parties will be privileged (a "Kovel" letter)
- Outlines the terms on which the appraiser would be involved in the event the IRS questions the valuation
- The approach taken to valuation
- The responsibilities of each party

What is a qualified appraisal?
- Made no earlier than 60 days before the contribution and no later than the date the tax filing is due (plus any extensions, typically April 15 or October 15 for Form 1040)
- Prepared, signed and dated by a qualified appraiser
- Appraisal fee is not contingent upon the appraised value
- Appraisal fee is not part of the charitable deduction
- Conducted in accordance with generally accepted appraisal standards
- Discounts for lack of marketability and control must be specifically researched and justified for your specific property (generic, blanket figures like "25%" no longer fly)

What is inside a qualified appraisal?
- Description of property
- Its physical condition

- Date of the contribution
- The terms of the deal
- Name, address, and taxpayer ID of the appraiser and his employer
- Appraiser's qualifications, including education and experience
- Declaration by the appraiser that they are qualified to make this appraisal
- The terms of any agreement between the donor and the donee related to the use, sale, or disposition of the property
- Statement that appraisal was prepared for income tax purposes (do not repurpose appraisals made for other reasons).
- This appraiser's declaration must be verbatim from the tax code
- Date on which the property was valued
- The valuation effective date and its fair market value on the date of contribution
- Any comparable items considered
- Justification of fair market value, including discussion of valuation methods employed

Who is this qualified appraiser?

- Someone who has an earned appraisal designation from a relevant, recognized professional appraisal organization
- Regularly receives compensation for conducting appraisals
- Is qualified to appraise the specific property
- Is aware of the penalties for overvaluation

Who is not a qualified appraiser?

- Anyone prohibited from practicing before the IRS in the last three years
- The taxpayer claiming the deduction
- The donor or whoever received the donation
- Any party to the property transfer
- Any person employed by or related to any of the above
- An appraiser who regularly appraises property for the donor who does not perform the majority of appraisals for other people

# In Sum

It can be complicated to claim a tax deduction for donating tangible property to charity. Read the IRS publications covering the type of property you want to donate, and bring in the right people (attorneys, appraisers, accountants) to advise you as the dollar amounts climb. If the process is not expensive, you are probably using the wrong people. Review the paperwork yourself to make sure it is accurate, complete, and consistent. If it doesn't make sense to you, why would a knowledgeable IRS agent take a different view? Remember, the IRS is devoting over $30 billion of its new revenues to enforcement, and the agency hates it when people try to claim excessive valuations on property.

# Chapter Ten

# Investing for Charity

A 2020 article by Lo, Matveyev, and Zeume at MIT looked at the investments from all U.S. nonprofit organizations over eight years. The average annual return on their invested capital (net of administrative expenses) was 5.3%. These non-profits should fire their investment advisors and place their endowments in an S&P 500 index fund, where they would have earned 11.2% a year over the same period—a performance improvement of 111%.

As individuals, most of us are accustomed to investing for retirement. This task requires great care since you do not want to run out of money late in life after you have become unemployable. Investing for charity is different. When you are investing money that you have earmarked for charity, there is no need to guard against a loss of income year-to-year. You can let the charity shoulder the volatility in exchange for the greater expected long-term returns that come from not sand-bagging the portfolio with low-performing investments. You don't need a "60/40" stock/bond portfolio. You can go all-in on stocks. You can even leverage the stocks if you know what you are doing.*

If you are investing for charity on your own, consider a one-ticker portfolio: VT, the Vanguard Total World Stock Fund.

From the Prospectus:

> The Fund employs an indexing investment approach designed to track the performance of the FTSE Global All-Cap index…9,526 stocks of of companies located in 49 markets, including both developed and emerging markets.

For an annual fee of 0.07%, this fund delivers the global stock market on a platter.

If international diversification holds no charms for you, the S&P 500 Index also stands ready to serve as a proxy for the U.S. stock market (ticker: VOO for Vanguard's exchange-traded fund, one among many for this index).

---

* But why stop there? See "Levering Up to Do Good" by Krasner, Liberman, Sosner and Brenner, *Journal of Beta Investment Strategies*, Fall 2024.

The only other asset you need is cash, which should be held to cover near-term expenses, such as charitable donations you expect to make over the next few years. Since stocks can lose 20% or more of their value on any given bad day, set aside cash for short-term commitments so you don't have to sell stocks when they are beaten down.

However, if you are investing in a legal structure that has any combination of income and charity beneficiaries—such as CLATs and CRUTs—I would encourage a moment of circumspection. You have a fiduciary duty to all trust beneficiaries. A family-member trustee might be inclined to privilege family beneficiaries over the charity beneficiaries. This would be wrong.

The first thing to do when investing in a trust is to examine the trust documents to learn how it defines trust income. Does trust income include capital gains, or not? This could have a big impact on your investing decisions, depending on your preference for dividends and interest vs. capital gains (for "total return") income.

Trustees are subject to the Prudent Investor Act of 1992, which took a "total portfolio" approach and says trustees should sell and diversify any private holdings as soon as possible. Most donor-advised funds and other charities will sell any securities you donate immediately.

If you are seeding a charitable trust with an illiquid asset that must be held rather than sold—perhaps a family business—the trust should be drafted with specific language allowing for the retention of the concentrated position, provide the rationale for it, and exculpate the trustees for not following the Prudent Investor Act.

In retrospect, even a portfolio that owned essentially every stock in the world (such as VT, above) could appear to be under diversified if the world stock market has a bad run. A beneficiary might sue because the investor failed to diversify into bonds. In other words, whatever happens over a trust's lifetime, a counterfactual portfolio can always be imagined *ex post* that would have done better for either the charity or the human beneficiaries. Absent malfeasance, charities will probably be forgiving. But what about your nephew? The joke in the estate planning business is that the first job is to identify the child who is level-headed and responsible, and the second is to identify the one who will be unhappy and sue. If you are investing for multiple beneficiaries with competing interests, some of whom might be litigious, a fund like Vanguard's LifeStrategy Moderate Growth Fund (ticker: VSMGX) delivers a globally diversified 60/40 stock/bond index portfolio for only 0.13% in annual expenses. To me, it would seem very difficult for a disgruntled beneficiary to claim that the trustee had failed to exercise fiduciary responsibility to diversify using a fund like this. Ideally, you could try to get buy-in to whatever investment strategy you propose by all affected parties.

When investing inside a charity structure (even one you might control, such as a family foundation), avoid any "jeopardizing" investments that can make you look imprudent:

- Trading on margin
- Commodity futures
- Working interests in oil and gas wells
- Puts, calls, straddles
- Selling short

When investing a Charitable Lead Annuity Trust, remember that the CLAT is not a charity. Either the donor (if a grantor trust) or the trust (if a nongrantor trust) will pay capital gains taxes on the asset sales inside the trust. Any income realized beyond covering the annuity or other expenses amounts to an unnecessary tax burden. A zero-dividend stock like Berkshire Hathaway would let you sell the minimum to cover these pay-outs without generating needless taxes. Low-expense U.S. stock market index exchange-traded funds (like VOO, mentioned above) are also relatively tax-friendly. Note: I have no financial relationship with Vanguard.

## Self-Dealing

. . . is defined as transactions between a "disqualified person" and a private foundation. Who are these disqualified persons? They include the founders and their family members, substantial contributors, the directors and officers, businesses owned by any of the above, as well as government officials.

Typically, these transactions include exchanges or leasing of property, loans, outright compensation, furnishing goods and services, and transfers of assets, even if these occur through intermediaries. Suppose you, the founder, want to sell your Gulfstream Jet to your private foundation for one dollar. Would that be considered self-dealing? Yes. It matters not whom the transaction benefits; penalties can apply.

**Investing within Donor-Advised Funds**

Here are my recommendations for investing in the big three donor-advised funds:

| TABLE 10.1: Rx Investments for Donor-Advised Funds | |
| --- | --- |
| **Vanguard** | **Expense Ratio** |
| Total Equity | 0.040% |
| (or) Total U.S. Stock Market | 0.020% |
| (or) S&P 500 | 0.020% |
| **Fidelity** | **Expense Ratio** |
| Total Market Index Pool | 0.015% |
| **Schwab** | **Expense Ratio** |
| Total Market Equity Index Pool | 0.030% |

Except for Vanguard, these charities would much prefer that you park your money in their more expensive actively managed mutual funds. But any of the funds in Table 10.1 will be fine for 100% of your long-term charitable dollars.

Fidelity buries its U.S. index fund option. When you open your account, keep clicking through the menu until you find the "Total Market Index Pool." Don't be misled by funds with similar names. The acid test is the low 0.015% expense ratio.

# Direct Indexing

Direct indexing lets you buy and hold, for example, every stock in the S&P 500 Index as opposed to purchasing an S&P 500 index fund. Because direct indexing enables you to do tax-loss harvesting on a company-by-company basis, it should be more tax-efficient than the index fund. However, the fees are still high for this service (which should be completely automated and free or nearly free), so you may not come out ahead vs. using a cheaper, tax-efficient exchange-traded index fund.

My concern about direct indexing for charitable donations of appreciated stock is that if you are constantly pruning your portfolio to give away the biggest winners, all this "lopping off their heads" might have a deleterious effect on your portfolio's performance. If they are rebuying these securities, where is the cash coming from to fund these purchases? If it comes from selling the other stocks in the portfolio and recognizing capital gains, what was the point of direct indexing? I would look forward to an academic study of this, especially one that is not paid for by the people selling direct indexing.

Until these issues are sorted out, owning a market-wide index-based exchange-traded fund bought over time might work better. That way, when you donate to charity, you could comb through the share lots to pick the ones with the lowest cost basis.

This lets you make contributions with the highest tax advantage without doing damage to the asset allocation of your portfolio.

# ESG Investing

Some people have the idea that, since they are investing for charity, for the sake of consistency they ought to follow an "ESG" (Environmental, Social, Governance) investing strategy. I have no wish to be polemical, but I feel obligated to outline the issues here.

Cliff Asness of AQR Capital, which sells ESG investing funds (among many others), has written a paper on the topic, "Virtue is its Own Reward or One Man's Ceiling is Another Man's Floor."

To summarize:

- Constraints, such as ESG screens, cannot improve expected investing returns. If they could, they would be desired by all investors seeking to maximize returns and not be constraints at all.
- When ESG investors avoid certain stocks, the market must still clear. Non-ESG investors ("sinners") must be induced to hold more of these stocks, which is achieved through lower stock prices and, therefore, higher expected returns.
- The higher expected returns for "sin stocks" translate to higher costs of capital for "sinful" companies. This results

in fewer "sinful" projects being approved, as fewer projects will have positive net present values.

- However, ESG investors must accept the "suck" of lower expected returns to achieve their goals. "Sinful" investors benefit from higher expected returns.

Unfortunately, Wall Street too often uses ESG as a gimmick to charge higher fees for worse performance, while implying that you might be rewarded with better returns by following their virtue-signaling strategies—although in this case, you may be primarily signaling your virtue to yourself. In other words, ESG can be a sales buzzword for an investment fad that is easy to get locked into but difficult to exit.

As Adam Smith wrote in the most famous paragraph in all of economics—the same one where he revealed the "invisible hand" back in 1776:

> "I have never known much good done by those who affected to trade for the public good."

My advice is to skip the ESG investing, buy the entire stock market, avoid the extra ongoing commissions to Wall Street, and deploy the extra money you earn on the causes that are important to you.

# Chapter Eleven

# Three Scenarios for
## Tax Strategy

*"We make a living by what we get, but we make a life by what we give."*

– Winston Churchill

This is the most important chapter for gaining a practical perspective on optimized lifetime giving.

Let me introduce the book's key metric, which I call *Giving Power*. I use it to evaluate the tax efficiency of charitable donations. *Giving Power equals your tax saving divided by the total amount donated to charity.*

If it only costs $80 after-tax to give $100 to charity, this equals a Giving Power of 20% (the $20 tax saving/$100 donation). The higher the Giving Power, the more we are leveraging the tax code to boost our charity dollars. The key is that this lets us compare how tax-effective we might be across different giving scenarios. It allows us to compare giving one way vs. giving another way today, or compare giving today vs. giving tomorrow, so we can pick our best spots to optimize our effectiveness. I believe that Giving Power can be sufficiently useful that you might want to retrofit your lifetime charitable giving strategy in its light.

Giving Power can be positive or negative since the tax code can work for you or against you. The last thing you want to do is pay extra taxes when you give to charity. You want to arrange your giving so you pay less tax, not more.

Imagine a genie handed you a list of the ten best and worst years to be in the stock market coming up over your lifetime. This would dramatically affect how you invest. You would not be a "buy-and-hold" investor, doing the same thing year after year. There would be good years when you would be in the market up to your gills, and bad years when you would sell everything and play golf.

Unfortunately, this list does not exist. But your Giving Power can be anticipated well enough to be helpful—to you and your charities.

The simple Giving Power calculators used in this chapter are available on a Google Sheet you can download from my website:

http://www.phildemuth.com

An online version of the simple Giving Power calculator is also under development at ETFMathGuy's website, which currently hosts two retirement calculators.

https://etfmathguy.com/

While these calculators can be a source of ideas for your charity tax strategy, rely on your own legal, tax, and financial advisors before making any moves based on them. Sadly, what you won't find here are calculators for CRUTs and CLATs.

Let's follow someone over their life cycle and examine the pros and cons of the giving opportunities that arise. As you read through these illustrations, the penny will drop in the gumball machine of your brain. The application of the best practices sketched in previous chapters will become clear as plate glass.

# RENEE AT 22

Renee has just graduated from college. Her last act of charity was selling Girl Scout cookies back in grammar school. Now, she stares at a letter from her college inviting her to get involved in ye olde alum association, starting with a donation to the college fund. What are her options?

We have dwelt on four main approaches through this book:

*Cash:* a possibility. She has a checking account and a credit card.

*Investments:* Renee has no stocks, bonds, or real estate. She has a trunk full of used college textbooks, but none are first editions by F. Scott Fitzgerald or Ernest Hemingway. Her art collection includes a Taylor Swift poster from her dorm room, not museum quality.

*Retirement Plan:* Renee opened a 401(k) at work, but she cannot (and should not) take money out of it, barring an emergency. Taxes and penalties would apply. This money is for retirement, and she remembers from Econ 101 that the secret is not to interrupt the compounding of her retirement savings.

*Estate:* Renee has no plans to die soon. She doesn't have a will, and considering her negative net worth (don't tell Dad about her credit card bill), she doesn't see the need for one.

Cash (or, worse, a credit card) is her only option. The problem is that she spends every dollar she earns and barely scrapes by as it is. She needs gas for her car and has a monthly car payment to make. She has a roommate and pays rent. She goes out with friends for drinks (expensive) and goes out to dinner with her posse every week. She buys clothes on eBay and from used ("vintage") clothing shops. She is in the market for a boyfriend. Giving money to her college is about the last thing on her mind. It can wait, possibly forever, but at least until her student loans are paid off.

In short, there is no evidence that Renee can afford to donate to charity.

If she did write a check to her alma mater, how much would it cost her?

| | TABLE 11.1: Gift of Cash |
|---:|:---|
| 22% | Marginal Federal Tax Rate |
| $15,000 | Standard Deduction (Single) |
| $0 | Other Schedule A Deductions |
| $100 | Donation to Registered Public Charity |
| -$22 | Federal Tax Savings |
| $122 | After-tax cost of Donation |
| **-22%** | **Giving Power** |

Her best opportunity is to spend $122 after-tax dollars to make a charitable contribution of $100, for an overall negative Giving Power: -22%. *For a cash giver who does not itemize deductions, Giving Power always equals the negative of their marginal tax rate.* Renee's intuition that this is the wrong time to be thinking about charity is correctly reinforced by the tax code. She should worry instead about getting out of debt. Our advice: just walk away Renee from this solicitation.

Exciting plot twist: Some scientists believe that our universe may be merely one of an infinite number of universes inside a big cosmic multiplex. Assuming this is true, let us contemplate our original Renee's situation in another universe identical in all respects to ours, except for the fact that in this universe, she is poor. We'll call this the "Poor Renee" storyline.

# POOR RENEE AT 22

At age 22, Poor Renee finds herself as a high school dropout who throws pots to sell at a local arts and crafts fair on Sunday mornings. Her revenues are about $100 on a good week. She lives in her parents' basement, and both she and they would prefer for her to move out but that is not in the cards. She fires her creations in a friend's kiln. She has no health insurance. What she really needs are marketable skills to open the door to higher-paid, full-time employment.

*Cash*: No cash

*Investments*: No investments.

*Retirement Plan*: No retirement plan.

*Estate*: No estate.

In short, charity is not top-of-mind for Poor Renee right now.

Finally, in this mind-bending science-fiction saga we have embarked upon, just one more multiverse over, lives Rich Renee.

# RICH RENEE AT 22

Rich Renee, age 22, is the lead vocalist in a rock'n'roll band. Thanks to early hits taking her to the toppermost of the poppermost, she has a net worth of $3 million. She has been too busy touring to spend it. Her agent thinks a million-dollar gift to an environmental charity could help her win a Grammy. He hauls in her business manager for a meeting.

*Cash:* Yes, Rich Renee has cash flow, but it's mostly tied up right now.

*Investments:* Yes, her business manager has hired an investment advisor who has put Renee in an investment portfolio. None of them has ever looked at her statements. For real estate, she lives in West Hollywood, but it's a rental.

*Retirement Plan:* Yes, a solo 401(k), same manager as above, untouchable.

*Estate Plan:* Yes, she has a will. Her money goes to her parents.

Her business manager explains that while Rich Renee is off to a great start, most performers have short careers and fail to save and invest for the long run. While in theory, a 22-year-old with $3 million. who lives modestly should be set for life, in practice, most celebrities in her position are broke within five years.

They decide to compromise: a $100,000 gift. They call Rich
Renee's publicist to set up a press conference.

But wait—how should Rich Renee make the gift?

| | TABLE 11.2: Gift of $100,000 Stock |
|---:|:---|
| 37.0% | Federal Tax Rate |
| 23.8% | Capital Gains Rate |
| $15,000 | Standard Deduction (Single) |
| $10,000 | Other Schedule A Deductions (Mortgage, SALT, etc.) |
| $100,000 | Charitable Donation |
| $5,000 | Capital Gains in gift |
| $31,450 | Income Taxes Saved |
| $1,190 | Capital Gains Taxes Saved |
| $36,340 | Total Taxes Saved |
| $63,660 | After-tax cost of Donation |
| **$36.3%** | **Giving Power** |

By giving appreciated stock, Renee—who understands
nothing of this—can double-dip, saving both on the capital
gains tax (because the charity will pay no taxes on the donated
appreciated securities) and the income tax (since the $100,000
donation is much larger than her standard deduction). The
downside is that she has owned the stocks for a short time, so
they only have 5% attached in the way of capital gains ($5,000
on a $100,000 investment). Still, all in, this buys $100,000 worth

of charity (plus the publicity) for $63,660, for an impressive Giving Power of 36.3%.

Her business manager has a daring idea. He will write off the charitable deduction as part of the publicity campaign for her album, a green-themed bash she is throwing. By donating from Rich Renee's personal corporation, $100,000 will disappear from her earnings. I cannot swear the IRS will love this. It would only cost her $63,000 to make a $100,000 charitable donation for an even higher Giving Power of 37%.

| | TABLE 11.3: Gift from LLC |
|---|---|
| 37.0% | Marginal Tax Bracket |
| N/A | Standard Deduction (Single) |
| $100,000 | Donation to Registered Public Charity |
| $37,000 | Federal Tax Savings |
| $63,000 | After-tax cost of Donation |
| **37%** | **Giving Power** |

*What We Learn from the Three Renees at 22:*

Unless they are rich, young people are not set up to give to charity. They should wait until their financial lives are on track and they can use the tax code to their advantage. But notice how a rich young person can stumble onto advisors who have ideas in this area.

# RENEE #1 AT 35

Back in our universe, you will be pleased to learn that Renee #1 picked up a husband, Joshua, and has a kid, Baby Leroy. They live in a pleasant valley suburb in a starter house where the kid can go to a "good" public school and have a free public school ride all the way through Rydell High.

Renee #1 stares at the annual letter she receives from her college development office (after homecoming weekend).

*Cash:* is still a possibility. She and her husband have a checking account and are rich in credit cards.

*Investments:* Joshua has recently opened a brokerage account. It holds an S&P 500 index fund worth $6,000. There was more, but they had to come up with a down payment for the house (with help from both their parents).

*Retirement Plan:* Yes, both Renee and Josh have 401(k) plans at work. These have been the main vehicle for their savings, probably because they work on autopilot, extracting and investing money from their paychecks. These are for retirement, not for charity. Using them would entail taxes and penalties.

*Estate:* When Baby Leroy came along, they drafted a will. Since dying is not an option, they bought term life insurance. But there is no room for charity in their estate at this point.

As Renee #1 reflects on her lack of ability to give, she finds herself at a different life stage but still in approximately the same position she was in 15 years earlier. Every dollar is spoken for. Their only "charity" is setting up a 529 plan to fund Baby Leroy's college education. Oh, and she's pregnant again.

Let's look at her Giving Power:

| TABLE 11.4: Gift of Cash | |
|---:|:---|
| 24% | Marginal Federal Tax Rate |
| $30,000 | Standard Deduction (Married Filing Jointly) |
| $17,000 | Other Schedule A Deductions |
| $1,000 | Donation to Registered Public Charity |
| -$240 | Federal Tax Savings |
| $1,240 | After-tax cost of Donation |
| **-24%** | **Giving Power** |

Yes, her Giving Power at age 35 is even worse than it was at age 22. She has climbed into a higher tax bracket, has a higher standard deduction to cross, and still has no surplus capital for charitable purposes.

What about that $6,000 in the index fund in their brokerage account, (i.e., their emergency account)? Are there any angles they could work, assuming they came to the unlikely conclusion that this was a good idea? Let's say they wanted to give $1,000 to charity. The money has not been in the account for long, so let's say that $1,000 has accumulated $100 in capital gains.

| | |
|---:|:---|
| **TABLE 11.5:** | |
| **Gift of Appreciated Stock** | |
| 24% | Marginal Federal Tax Rate |
| 15.0% | Capital Gains Bracket |
| $30,000 | Standard Deduction (Married Filing Jointly) |
| $17,000 | Other Schedule A Deductions |
| $1,000 | Donation to Registered Public Charity |
| $100 | Capital Gains in donated securities |
| $0 | Income Taxes Saved |
| $15 | Capital Gains Taxes Avoided |
| $15 | Federal Tax Savings |
| $985 | After-tax cost of Donation |
| **1.5%** | **Giving Power** |

The best that can be said is that the 1.5% Giving Power in this example is better than the –24% giving from their checkbook. They are going to pass on the current giving opportunities.

# POOR RENEE AT 35

. . . has landed a position with the city as one of the organizers of the Sunday Market. It pays her $19,000 a year—no benefits—and she can still sell her pots at a friend's booth. She can also buy produce from the farmers' stands at a discount, a perk, although it still costs three times as much as shopping at Kroger's.

She lives at her boyfriend's apartment. He's hot but not what you'd call a great provider. It's not clear where this relationship is going. He talks about moving back to Ontario but has never explicitly said she is invited.

*Cash*: de minimis.

*Investments*: None

*Retirement Plan*: None.

*Estate*: None.

*Options for Charitable Giving:* No financial options available. But Poor Rene gets a brainwave: she suggests to the Market organizers that they devote a free booth every Sunday to a local charity to promote the charity's pledge drive or other programs. Everyone thinks this is a terrific idea, so they put her in charge of it. Poor Renee's new superpower enables her to reach out to all the local charities, who, in turn, have every reason to be nice to her.

## RICH RENEE AT 35

. . . has made the transition from the music business to film. Her initial star turn in *Devil Girl from Alcatraz* went well, and now she has several offers in her inbox. Her quote is $3 million per project.

*Cash*: yes, lots.

Rich Renee has acquired some other Schedule A deductions that might make a below-the-line cash gift work better than last time.

| | TABLE 11.6: Gift of Cash |
|---:|:---|
| 37% | Marginal Federal Tax Rate |
| $15,000 | Standard Deduction (Single) |
| $20,000 | Other Schedule A Deductions |
| $100,000 | Donation to Registered Public Charity |
| $37,000 | Federal Tax Savings |
| $63,000 | After-tax cost of Donation |
| **37%** | **Giving Power** |

She could try donating from her corporation, perhaps hosting a cocktail party for the environmental charity and claiming it as a marketing or publicity expense "above-the-line" like she tried last time.

| | TABLE 11.7: Gift from LLC |
|---:|:---|
| 37.0% | Marginal Tax Bracket |
| N/A | Standard Deduction (Single) |
| $100,000 | Donation to Registered Public Charity |
| $37,000 | Federal Tax Savings |
| $63,000 | After-tax cost of Donation |
| **37%** | **Giving Power** |

The $100,000 donation from her LLC costs her $63,000 in after-tax income for a Giving Power of 37%—the same as giving from her checkbook. While this does not work better for federal taxes, it would help with her state taxes (not shown).

However, that won't be necessary because there is a still better way open to her.

*Investments:* Rich Renee owns a house in Laurel Canyon and a diversified portfolio of stocks and bonds. Her S&P 500 Index fund has doubled in value since she bought it over ten years ago. Let's compare this with the cash gift:

| | TABLE 11.8: Gift of $100,000 Stock |
|---:|:---|
| 37.0% | Fed Tax Bracket |
| 23.8% | Capital Gains Bracket |
| $15,000 | Standard Deduction |
| $20,000 | Other Schedule A Deductions (Mortgage, SALT) |
| $100,000 | Charitable Donation |
| $50,000 | Capital Gains in gift |
| $37,000 | Income Taxes Saved |
| $11,900 | Capital Gains Taxes Saved |
| $48,900 | Total Taxes Saved |
| $51,100 | After-tax cost of Donation |
| **48.9%** | **Giving Power** |

To heck with giving from her checkbook or her LLC. Rich Renee is better off double-dipping into the tax code for an income and capital gains tax break by donating appreciated stock to charity instead. That way, the same $100,000 contribution only costs her $51,100 for an impressive Giving Power of 49%.

*Retirement Plan*: yes, a solo 401(k) from her corporation, and no need to touch it at this point.

*Estate*: She has not revised her estate plan, and charity is not a part of it. It could be, but she is afraid if she touches her estate plan, she will die.

*What We Learn from the Three Renees at 35:*

Even well into midlife, most people will not be able to give to charity with much of an assist from Uncle Sam unless they are high income or rich. They do better by waiting for an opportunity later. This is the numbers talking.

# RENEE #1 AT 50

Renee #1 and husband Joshua survey their financial lives. They have both done well in their careers. They have a brokerage account on top of their 401(k) plans. Their financial advisor has run a report that shows their retirement savings are on track. It looks like they can afford to give to charity.

Renee stares at this year's appeal from her college development office. Baby Leroy, now 18, will be applying, and her daughter Lola will follow in his footsteps soon after that. It can't hurt for the family to be on the list of donors. What should they do?

*Cash*: There is cash in the checking account.

Giving Power at Age 50:

| | TABLE 11.9: Gift of $5,000 Cash |
|---:|:---|
| 32% | Fed Tax Bracket |
| $30,000 | Standard Deduction (Married Filing Jointly) |
| $20,000 | Other Schedule A Deductions (Mortgage, SALT) |
| $5,000 | Charitable Donation |
| ($1,600) | Federal Tax Savings |
| $6,600 | After-tax cost of Donation |
| **-32%** | **Giving Power** |

Their high tax bracket, coupled with the fact that the gift is not enough to overcome the standard deduction, means this is an expensive way to give. Next!

*Stocks*: There are appreciated stocks in their brokerage account.

The earliest shares of the index fund they bought have grown to where about half their holdings consist of capital gains. If they donated these directly to the college:

| | TABLE 11.10: Gift of $5,000 Stock |
|---:|---|
| | **TABLE 11.10:**<br>**Gift of $5,000 Stock** |
| 32% | Fed Tax Bracket |
| 18.3% | Capital Gains Bracket |
| $30,000 | Standard Deduction (Married Filing Jointly) |
| $20,000 | Other Sched. A Deductions |
| $5,000 | Donation to Registered Public Charity |
| $2,500 | Capital Gains in donated securities |
| $0 | Income Taxes Saved |
| $458 | Capital Gains Taxes Saved |
| $458 | Federal Tax Savings |
| $4,543 | After-tax cost of Donation |
| **9.2%** | **Giving Power** |

That night, Renee #1 has a dream: The Director of Admissions is having lunch with the Head of the College Development Office. Buttering his roll, the director happens to drop that Renee—an alum—has a son applying for admission.

"What a coincidence," replies the development officer, "we just received a handsome check from the family."

"Hmm," says the admissions director, chewing thoughtfully, "They must truly be committed to the school. Maybe we should overlook Leroy's disappointing Math SAT score and consider the whole child. . . ."

As she wakes up, Renee's mind starts racing. If Baby Leroy gets in, his sister will apply two years later. If they give $5,000 three years in a row, this might appear to the school as an immutable pattern that will go on forever. Lola, a legacy applicant with an attending brother from a donor family, would have every chance of getting in. Who knows, the grateful college might become a "family school" for generations.

They run this idea by their financial planner, who suggests putting $15,000 in a donor-advised fund today and parceling the money out to the college over three years. "Inside the donor-advised fund, the college won't know how much money you've got. They might assume there are millions of dollars sloshing around. Maybe they'll think you could put your name on the new football stadium." Lulled into complacency after cashing these checks three years in a row, the college development office will never foresee that once Lola is admitted, their gravy train will come crashing to a stop.

After running the numbers, this stock gift idea looks even better:

The bigger charitable gift bunched into one year, on top of their $10,000 mortgage deduction and $10,000 state tax deduction, pushes them over the standard deduction by $5,000. Itemizing their deductions on Schedule A saves them $1,600 in income taxes in addition to the $1,410 they save on capital gains taxes. They do the income tax/capital tax gains double dip for a very respectable 20.1% giving power—much better than the 9.2% Giving Power they would get from donating $5,000 worth of stock as originally planned.

| | TABLE 11.11: Gift of $15,000 Stock |
|---|---|
| 32% | Fed Tax Bracket |
| 18.8% | Capital Gains Bracket |
| $30,000 | Standard Deduction (Married Filing Jointly) |
| $20,000 | Other Schedule A Deductions (Mortgage, SALT) |
| $15,000 | Charitable Donation |
| $7,500 | Capital Gains in gift |
| $1,600 | Income Taxes Saved |
| $1,410 | Capital Gains Taxes Avoided |
| $3,010 | Total Taxes Saved |
| $11,990 | After-tax cost of Donation |
| **20.1%** | **Giving Power** |

They are about to wrap up the meeting with their financial planner when Josh pipes up. "You know, I seem to remember that my company has some kind of corporate match. I don't suppose it would cover anything like this. Would it be worth a phone call to HR to find out?"

Renee and the planner look at him in disbelief.

It turns out his corporation offers a 100% match, up to an annual limit of $2,500. Giving to schools is fine. Giving from a donor-advised fund is fine.

A week later, they huddle again in the planner's office. The new printout looks like table 11.12, and it covers three years of $5,000 donations.

| | TABLE 11.12: Stock Gift + Employer Match |
|---|---|
| 32% | Fed Tax Bracket |
| 18.3% | Capital Gains Bracket |
| $30,000 | Standard Deduction |
| $20,000 | Other Sched. A Deductions |
| $7,500 | Donation to Registered Public Charity |
| $3,750 | Capital Gains in donated secutities |
| $0 | Income Taxes Saved |
| $686 | Capital Gains Taxes Avoided |
| $686 | Federal Tax Savings |
| $6,814 | After-tax cost of Donation |
| **9.2%** | **Pre-Match Giving Power** |
| $7,500 | Employer Match |
| $15,000 | Total Donation |
| $6,814 | Total Cost of Donation |
| **55%** | **Giving Power** |

The total dollars to the college are the same, but the Giving Power is much higher because of the leverage from the employer match. The Giving Power from the Donor-Advised Fund fell from

22% to 9.2% because the smaller gift at their end meant they did not surpass the standard deduction. Their only benefit was the capital gains avoidance on the stock they donated. Even so, the 100% employer match made the plan work for half the original cost of the plan, which only posted a giving power of 20.1%. A Giving Power of 55% puts them in serious philanthropist territory.

*Retirement Plans*: Apart from the house, most of their savings are here. But tapping them would generate taxes and penalties. They are preserved for retirement.

*Estate*: They could spend thousands of dollars on legal fees to modify their estate plan to leave some money to the college, but how would that help Baby Leroy get into college next fall or his sister Lola a few years later?

# POOR RENEE AT 50

Poor Renee's Mom died this year, leaving her and her two siblings with the house. After the estate settles, she is left with $100,000. She meets a friendly stockbroker who talks her into buying an annuity that will pay her $500/month for the rest of her life.

The annuity will cover some of her basic living expenses, but there is nothing left over for charity.

While she has no good financial options for charity, her weekly charity booth at the Sunday market has worked well. Sometimes, she helps staff the table, pass out literature, and schmooze with the locals. More than once, she has introduced a new supporter to the charity-of-the-week from her social network around the market. She has become friends with several of the charity employees and participated in a walkathon and a blood drive. When disposing of her parents' furniture and possessions, she was able to triage the items to local charities.

# RICH RENEE AT 50

Too old to be a star, too young to be an institution, Renee badgers her agent for the occasional booking as an actor or singer to "reinvent" herself and reignite her career, but nothing has caught fire so far. All that stuff about "ageism" in Hollywood turns out to be true. Her time is increasingly devoted to charitable causes. She sat next to a venture capitalist at a fundraiser; he was a fan and now they plan to be married as soon as his divorce is finalized.

*What We Learn from the Three Renees at 50:*

Giving cash to charity is ordinarily suboptimal when it gets swallowed by the standard deduction. The exception would be if a generous employer match acts as a wild card for turbocharged

Giving Power. Rich people can give in whatever way they find most tax-effective at the time. *For most upper-middle-class earners, the earliest opportunity for tax-leveraged giving will be through donating stock from a taxable brokerage account, probably around midlife.* Even this assumes they are ahead of the game in funding their retirements. The stock should have significant capital gains, should be large enough (alongside the other itemized deductions) to eclipse the standard deduction, and should go to a donor-advised fund, allowing the givers to spread the subsequent donations to their end charities over time.

# RENEE #1 AT 65

Renee #1 and Joshua are going to retire this year and start Medicare. It's time to put up the periscope for a 360-degree look.

The kids are finished with school and are out of the home. They are healthy and employed. Mission accomplished. . . so far.

Renee and Josh's financial plans look like they have retirement covered, barring some calamity. They can always dial back spending if necessary.

What are their charitable giving options? Joshua's current job offers no employee match.

*Cash:* Since they are postponing Social Security until age 70, they will have no ordinary income for the next five years! While they could do a cash-based charitable gift with no income tax penalty, it is not that simple. Their planner wants them to use these low-tax years to do significant Roth conversions from their traditional retirement plans. The Roth conversions should reduce their tax bill over their entire retirement. But it will put them in the 22% bracket, which means a -22% Giving Power on cash contributions.

*Investments:* This looks more promising. There are stocks and mutual funds in the brokerage account that have been compounding for decades.

They can use their retirement accounts for tax-advantaged charitable giving once they turn 73 (or 75 for those born after 1959) and RMDs kick in. They are looking to inject 8 years of retirement giving (at $5,000/year) into their donor-advised fund today to tide them over until then.

Notice how the timing makes a difference:

If they make the gift while they are still working (peak earning years), it goes like this:

| | TABLE 11.13: Gift of Stock While Working |
|---:|:---|
| 32.0% | Fed Tax Bracket |
| 18.3% | Capital Gains Bracket |
| $33,200 | Standard Deduction (Married Filing Jointly> 65) |
| $10,000 | Other Schedule A Deductions (Mortgage, SALT) |
| $40,000 | Charitable Donation |
| $30,000 | Capital Gains in gift |
| $5,376 | Income Taxes Saved |
| $5,490 | Capital Gains Taxes Saved |
| $10,866 | Total Taxes Saved |
| $29,134 | After-tax cost of Donation |
| **27.2%** | **Giving Power** |

But if they wait until after they have retired, the picture isn't as pretty. Their only income is from doing Roth conversions, and these only take them into the 22% bracket.

| | TABLE 11.14: Gift of Stock When Retired |
|---:|:---|
| 22.0% | Fed Tax Bracket |
| 15.0% | Capital Gains Bracket |
| $33,200 | Standard Deduction (Married Filing Jointly > 65) |
| $10,000 | Other Schedule A Deductions (Mortgage, SALT) |
| $40,000 | Charitable Donation |

| | |
|---|---|
| $30,000 | Capital Gains in gift |
| $3,696 | Income Taxes Saved |
| $4,500 | Capital Gains Taxes Saved |
| $8,196 | Total Taxes Saved |
| $31,804 | After-tax cost of Donation |
| **20.5%** | **Giving Power** |

Giving Power math shows the best path. They can make the same $40,000 gift at a cost of $29,134 while working or $31,804 if they wait until after they retire.

*Retirement Plan:* While they can now pull money from their IRAs without penalty, every dollar counts as ordinary income, with a giving power equal to the negative of their marginal tax rate. It is the same as giving cash. From an overall planning perspective, it is much smarter to use these pre–Social Security, low-tax years to maximize Roth conversions. That opportunity won't come again. A point to keep in mind: it is counterproductive to convert any IRA dollars to Roth that are destined for charity.

*Estate:* They don't envision having a major estate. There will be no estate tax to avoid. They will leave whatever is left—their house and their retirement accounts—to their kids. They would rather give to charity while they are alive than give via their estate, especially with no estate tax to offset. If the kids want to give money they inherit to charity, that will be their call.

# POOR RENEE AT 65

Poor Renee's stint working for the city ended this year. It gave her enough employment credits to qualify for Social Security and Medicare. It isn't a lot of money, but cobbled together with her annuity and the other tax breaks for low-income people, she can get by. Outright cash gifts to charity are out of the question.

*Cash*: None to spare.

*Investments*: No real estate, stocks, or bonds.

*Retirement Plans*: Social Security + Annuity

*Estate Plan*: None

# RICH RENEE AT 65

Rich Renee's band (minus a couple of original members) will be performing in the Las Vegas Sphere for one month this year.

*Cash*: You bet. Best of all, the money comes in as carried interest from her husband's Venture Capital fund and gets taxed as capital gains, not ordinary income.

*Investments*: She and her husband, Zak, live in a $22 million house on the beach in Malibu. Zak's money is largely tied up in his companies, but there's enough left over to cover essentials. Renee still has her professionally managed investment accounts.

*Retirement Plans:* Yes. While Rich Renee has not contributed very much to her plans over the past decade, the core investments have been growing for a long time.

*Estate:* Renee and Zak went to an estate planning attorney in Century City. The final document is Greek to her. Zak has a trust that will take care of his kids from a previous marriage and another trust that will pay for Renee's lifestyle while she is alive.

Renee is increasingly active with charity work. Zak is happy because it keeps her occupied and out of his (thinning, graying) hair.

They funnel their charitable donations through their private foundation because their attorney suggested it and it sounded cool. Zak's kids are also on its board of directors, so maybe they are learning something. If Zak and Rich Renee took the trouble to run the numbers, they would see that their charitable giving could be handled more efficiently through a donor-advised fund coupled with direct gifts of appreciated stock.

*What We Learn from the Three Renees at 65:*

The planning opportunities in early retirement need to be carefully considered. Is it economically advantageous to do Roth conversions, and if so, when and how big—up to which tax threshold? Second, is there room to give to charity before retiring?

If your analysis shows that the taxable account will not be depleted over your retirement, the lowest-basis shares of stock will never be sold. Absent any write-off for savings on capital gains, this donation will not achieve the total "giving power" that you might attribute to them. You would do better to donate the funds with high expense ratios or the high dividend payers with more modest capital gains, or wait and do your charitable giving through your retirement plans later.

# RENEE #1 AT 73

Renee #1 and Joshua have spent down their Donor-Advised Fund to nothing, as planned. Their family's financial circumstances continue to be favorable, so they have a green light for more charitable giving.

*Cash*: Their cash donations have a Giving Power of −22%.

*Investments*: The stocks in their brokerage account have lower capital gains since they gave away the lowest-basis holdings to their donor-advised fund when they were sixty-five. But it is still worth running the numbers to be certain of the best option.

| | |
|---:|:---|
| **TABLE 11.15:** | |
| **Gift of $5,000 Stock** | |
| 22.0% | Fed Tax Bracket |
| 15.0% | Capital Gains Bracket |
| $33,200 | Standard Deduction (Married Filing Jointly) |
| $10,000 | Other Schedule A Deductions (Mortgage, SALT) |
| $5,000 | Charitable Donation |
| $2,500 | Capital Gains in gift |
| $0 | Income Taxes Saved |
| $375 | Capital Gains Taxes Saved |
| $375 | Total Taxes Saved |
| $4,625 | After-tax cost of Donation |
| **7.5%** | **Giving Power** |

*Retirement Plans*: They started Social Security at age 70. Now they are 73 and can pull out Qualified Charitable Distributions from their IRAs. Every dollar they donate cancels out a dollar of their required minimum distributions.

| | |
|---:|:---|
| **TABLE 11.16:** | |
| **Gift of IRA Qualified Charitable Distribution** | |
| 22% | Fed Marginal Tax Bracket |
| $50,000 | Required Minimum Distribution |
| $5,000 | Charitable Donation |
| $1,100 | Federal Tax Savings |
| $3,900 | After-tax cost of Donation |
| **22%** | **Giving Power** |

This time, the gift—starting from the first dollar—comes out at their marginal tax rate.

If they had chosen to make the gift to their donor-advised fund in the form of appreciated stock, they would have to give over $55,000 to achieve the same effective Giving Power. But as retirees, they are disinclined to make large one-time purchases (including bunching contributions for charity). They prefer the optionality that comes from making smaller annual gifts from their IRAs.

*Estate:* While a taxable estate is not envisioned, the question of whether to draw charitable dollars from the Donor-Advised Fund vs. taking Qualified Charitable Distributions from their IRA accounts has estate planning implications.

The money inside their IRAs (rolled over from their 401(k) plans) is, of course, pretax. It is going to come out of their IRAs at some point: either at Renee #1 and Joshua's tax rate today, or tomorrow after one of them dies and the surviving spouse is filing "single"—possibly into higher tax brackets—or, worst of all, as inherited IRAs paid out to their children during their kids' peak earning years. For people with charitable intent, these IRA dollars are the ones to donate first (assuming the planned Roth conversions were completed earlier). Meanwhile, the stocks in the brokerage account will be taxed more lightly as they are drawn out over time (at capital gains rates vs. ordinary income rates), will receive a step-up in basis in their community property state when the first spouse passes, and then receive a second step-up basis when the surviving spouse dies before going to Leroy and Lola. There is no reason to draw these down. Finally, their Roth IRAs contain posttax dollars. These offer no Giving Power, and the Roths are the last money to be spent because they are even more valuable to their affluent kids.

## POOR RENEE AT 73

Poor Renee's straightened financial circumstances leave her with no financial assets to donate to charity. If truth be told, the Rich Renees and Renee #1s of her universe end up transferring some of their money to her via government tax and transfer social programs.

While Renee was disappointed in some of the charity people who ghosted her the minute she no longer had a free booth at the market to give away, others had become good friends. She spends a couple of days every week doing part-time volunteer work at their organizations.

# RICH RENEE AT 73

Renee's husband's venture capital firm plans to spin out one of its portfolio companies in an initial public offering, and this gives Renee an idea.

They happen to have an expensive 100-page expert appraisal of the company they showed to the investment bank to justify an IPO price of $10/share (vs. their cost basis of $0.50/share). Why don't they take this same report across the street to their donor-advised fund and tell them they want to donate 100,000 shares of the pre-IPO company to their DAF account? It could be worth a $1,000,000 charitable deduction. The DAF could sell the stock at the opening. Since Renee and her husband are minority shareholders, they are entitled to donate their shares to charity.

Unexpectedly, the DAF is not wild about an appraisal not prepared for tax purposes. They tell Rich Renee that the IRS will take a 20% haircut off the appraised value for lack of marketability and control. The stock might be worth $1,000,000 at the IPO, but as of today, there is no market and the IPO remains hypothetical, as does the price. Even if they settle on a $800,000 valuation for the stock, if it opens at $600,000, the IRS will regard it with suspicion. Meanwhile, if it opened at $1,200,000, they would still be stuck with the $800,000 valuation.

Rich Renee and her husband confer and decide to come back 90 days after the IPO. Now, there is a market and a price; the DAF accepts and sells the shares for $1,000,000 and deposits the proceeds into their account. Everyone is happy.

| | TABLE 11.17: Gift of Stock |
|---:|:---|
| 37.0% | Fed Tax Bracket |
| 23.8% | Capital Gains Bracket |
| $33,200 | Standard Deduction (Married Filing Jointly > 65) |
| $21,000 | Other Schedule A Deductions (Mortgage, SALT) |
| $1,000,000 | Charitable Donation |
| $950,000 | Capital Gains in gift |
| $365,486 | Income Taxes Saved |
| $226,100 | Capital Gains Taxes Saved |
| $591,586 | Total Taxes Saved |
| $408,414 | After-tax cost of Donation |
| **59.2%** | **Giving Power** |

*What we Learn from the Three Renees at 73:*

This example highlights how making large gifts on highly tax-advantageous terms is the preserve of the wealthy. *For the rest of us, Qualified Charitable Distributions from IRA accounts become the go-to giving vehicle of choice for retirees.* These let people make annually adjustable donations while (a) sidestepping the haircut from the standard deduction, (b) lowering ordinary income to help avoid various tax land mines, and (c) spending down the least desirable part of their estate to pass along to their children.

# RENEE #1 IN OLD AGE

Renee #1 and Joshua look back on their lives and reflect on how it continues to be true that any cash gifts they make to charity in their old age still have a Giving Power (now a Giving Penalty) equal to the negative of their tax rate.

In past years, they have donated appreciated stock and made qualified distributions from their IRA, all to good effect. Now the question is: is there any reason to consider giving from their estate?

With the joint estate-and-gift tax exemption set at $27.98 million, they are not going to pay estate taxes. There are no attractive 40% estate tax savings to harvest by donating part of their estate to charity.

They run the numbers on leaving an IRA to a Charity Remainder Unitrust (CRUT). Renee #1's IRA has been spent down over retirement, leaving a balance of $500,000.

The CRUT example here embodies real-world constraints. The kids have a twenty-seven-year joint life expectancy, and the Trustee correctly takes five of these years to transfer the assets into the CRUT, allowing the principal to grow tax-free during this period with no distributions. The Trustee also invests the money not in stocks, but in a balanced mutual fund with a classic 60/40 stock/bond allocation.

The CRUT distributions to the kids are taxed as ordinary income at the kids' 32% tax rate, where they continue to grow with no further management fees but now face investment taxes from the world outside the CRUT.

In the counter-example, the kids inherit the IRA directly and take ten years to drain it into their brokerage accounts. They invest in the same 60/40 fund and pay investment taxes along the way.

After 27 years, table 11.18 shows how it stands.

| TABLE 11.18: $500,000 CRUT vs. IRA to Kids | | |
|---|---|---|
| | CRUT | IRA |
| Charitable Deduction | $62,886 | $0 |
| Final Amount to Charity | $277,054 | $0 |
| CRUT Management Fee | 1% | N/A |
| Total $ to Kids | $1,201,012 | $1,507,556 |
| Cost of Charity Dollars | $306,544 | |
| **Giving Power** | **-11%** | |

Unfortunately, the kids end up with more money (and more control over the money and with less money lost to management fees) by inheriting directly: $1.5 million vs. $1.2 million. Worse, this difference in performance between the two approaches means that while there is $277,054 left inside the CRUT going to charity, these dollars cost more than the $306,544 lost to foregone investment performance. The Giving Power is –11 %. Nothing about this pencils out.

What are their other options? If Renee #1 and Joshua still wanted to give money to charity via their estate, they could either donate stocks from their brokerage account or name a charity as a beneficiary of their IRAs. Between these two choices, it is far better to leave the stocks and the house to the kids because the tax basis would be reset to fair market value. But the IRA, with its pretax income, would be taxed at Leroy and Lola's marginal tax rates, possibly even kicking them into a higher tax bracket.

It sinks in that their kids are now in a higher tax bracket than they are. Joshua gets an idea. He could convert his IRA to a Roth, paying the taxes at his lower rate. If he leaves them a Traditional IRA, the $500,000 will turn into $340,000 after they pay taxes on their withdrawals at 32%. But if he converts it to a Roth IRA in the 24% bracket, they will have $380,000 to spend. Of course, he will have to pay for the Roth conversion using outside funds, but the kids still come out ahead.

This is a no-brainer. He would have to do it over several years, skirting the top of the 24% tax bracket to avoid kicking them into the 32% tax bracket, which would negate the whole point of the exercise.

Renee pipes in with a helpful suggestion. "Honey, instead of paying taxes on the Roth conversion, can we just make a charitable donation instead?"

Joshua goes into his study, gets out a yellow legal pad and sharpens a pencil.

An hour later, the door to his study opens. "Yes, I am a genius. You may recall the Algebra prize I won in high school." He looks over at a small trophy on the fireplace mantel. "Here's what we're gonna do."

"Ideally, we would like to pay for the Roth with a Qualified Charitable Distribution from the IRA itself. But that can't work. Every dollar going to a QCD only pays for its own withdrawal."

"Then what's the answer?"

"We pay for the conversion from our taxable account, using appreciated stocks. We have to pay a bit more to top off our standard deduction before we get a dollar-for-dollar offset, but it's worth doing. The kids end up with more walking-around money after-tax, plus they get a kitty of $136,200 in the family DAF (see figure 11.19).

| | |
|---:|:---|
| | **TABLE 11.19:** |
| | **Convert IRA to Roth for Kids?** |
| | **Scenario 1: No Roth Conversion** |
| $500,000 | Parent's IRA |
| $500,000 | Parent's Taxable Account |
| 32% | Child's Marginal Tax Rate |
| $840,000 | Total After-Tax to Child |
| | **Scenario 2: Roth Conversion with Charitable Offset** |
| 24.0% | Parent's Marginal Tax Rate |
| $33,200 | Standard Deduction (Married Filing Jointly > 65) |
| $17,000 | Other Schedule A Deductions (Mortgage, SALT) |
| $136,200 | Charitable Donation |
| $863,800 | Total After-Tax to Child |
| **17.5%** | **Giving Power** |

Keep in mind:

- The owner should not convert to Roth any amount that is destined for their own consumption
- In the event that it takes multiple years to complete the conversion (due to bracket creep or AGI limits), Giving Power will be negatively affected by any recurring standard deduction shortfall
- The inheritors of the new Roth accounts should let them grow undisturbed for ten years instead of plundering them for immediate spending

# POOR RENEE IN OLD AGE

Poor Renee has no options for charitable giving beyond donating her organs and leaving her body to medical school after she passes. You might say, she gave everything she had. In the words of Warren Buffett: "These people receive no recognition whether they mentor the young, assist the elderly or devote precious hours to community betterment. They do not have buildings named after them, but they silently make those establishments—schools, hospitals, churches, libraries, whatever—work smoothly."*

---

* Over dinner at Piccolo's in Omaha, I asked Mr. Buffett whether he ever called up Bill Gates to say something like, "Bill, I saw an interesting new charity on page A6 of today's *Wall Street Journal*. You might want to check it out."

Warren looked at me with great concern.

Warren: "No. I wouldn't dream of doing that. Not in a million years."

Phil: "But—you've given him $37 billion. He'll take your call!"

Warren: "You don't hire a plumber and then stand around telling him what to do."

# RICH RENEE IN OLD AGE

Thanks to the success of the Venture Capital firm, Rich Renee and her husband have an estate worth $30 million. In their community property state, Renee's share of this is $14.99 million, a bit over her Estate Tax Exemption of $13.99 million. Is there any way she can duck the 40% federal estate tax on the overage?

Yes! Rich Renee's retirement account is worth $3 million. Rich Renee shrewdly opens a new IRA, naming her family's donor-advised fund as the sole beneficiary, and then rolls over $1 million from her original IRA into it. The remaining $2 million in the IRA continues to go to the kids, just as before, but now will be free of estate taxes. Her total estate is worth $13.99 million, the exact amount of the estate tax exemption.

| | TABLE 11.20: Testamentary Gift of IRA |
|---:|:---|
| $14,990,000 | Initial Size of Estate |
| $13,990,000 | Estate Tax Exemption |
| 40% | Estate Tax Rate |
| $1,000,000 | Value of IRA Charitable Gift |
| $400,000 | Federal Estate Tax Saving |
| $600,000 | After-tax cost of Donation |
| **40%** | **Giving Power** |

The 40% giving power comes entirely from ducking the federal estate tax that would otherwise be due on Renee's IRA assets that pushed her over the estate tax exemption. Gifts like this need to be planned in consultation with an estate attorney and tax advisors.

*What We Learn from the Three Renees in Old Age:*

When it comes to estate tax planning, start by leaving the IRAs to charity.

## The Longitudinal View

Looking over the highest Giving Power examples from Renee #1 and Rich Renee over the decades, what do we notice?

| TABLE 11.21: Maximum Giving Power | | |
|---|---|---|
| Age | Renee #1 | Rich Renee |
| 22 | -22% | 37% |
| 35 | 2% | 49% |
| 50 | 55% | NA |
| 65 | 30% | NA |
| 72 | 22% | 59% |
| 95 | 18% | 40% |

Look at the wide range of leverage available at these different life passages: for Renee #1, from –22% to 55%. For Rich Renee, from 37% to 59%. The idea is to pick your shots: don't give when your Giving Power is low or negative; give big when Uncle Sam donates with you.

Apart from access to a generous employer match, people who are affluent but not rich (Renee #1) will not find their Giving Power flaming on until later in their careers. Earlier, their salaries have not peaked (highest income tax = potentially highest Giving Power) and the securities in their brokerage account have not had time to ripen with untaxed capital gains. Only their high-earning years allow for donations exceeding their standard deduction. While Giving Power recedes after switching to Qualified Charitable Distributions from Renee #1's IRA, it fits in very well with her overall financial plan at that point.

The rich are different. They have enough assets to make large gifts to charity even early in life. While Renee #1's average lifetime gift was $12,300, Rich Renee averaged $820,000. Large gifts get the biggest boost from the tax code because their deduction usually applies against the highest tax rates. Big charity is a rich person's sport. The rich have surplus capital, better advisors, and potentially the time and interest to see it wisely used. Because they start earlier, they have more opportunities to learn from early false starts, make course corrections, and give with increasing conviction and effectiveness over time.

# Chapter Twelve

# Life-Cycle Charitable **Planning**

*"Learn. Earn. Return."*

– Shelby Davis

Charitable giving is usually approached as something a person or family does the same way every year, or occurs circumstantially, in response to being asked to give. This book proposes a different paradigm for charitable giving—one that is more intentional and deliberate, possibly lifelong, and optimized along broadly utilitarian lines, using the tax code to obtain the greatest advantage.

In the 1950s, economist Franco Modigliani suggested that individuals should plan their finances to smooth out saving and spending over the life cycle. The big idea was that people should save and invest their surplus capital while young so they could spend down their accumulated savings over retirement, the mother of all financial liabilities—all while maintaining a more-or-less constant standard of living over their lifetimes. This insight was good enough for a Nobel Prize in 1985.

The giving scenarios we have just reviewed show how a similar process applies to charitable giving. First, it means comparing the giving opportunities available to you today to identify the one with the greatest Giving Power. Second, you could compare today's highest Giving Power idea with your prospects for giving in the future. Those might land in high income years, or when some special situation arises, or after you start taking required minimum distributions from your retirement accounts, or still later, giving through your estate.

Instead of donating the same dollars every year, no matter what your Giving Power is, the idea is to identify when you can "buy" the most charity per dollar with the finite charity dollars you have available, so you do the most good with what you have. At its simplest, Giving Power lets you compare the effectiveness of the charitable options available to you when the need arises. But its highest and best use would be to tailor your lifetime giving plan around your biggest Giving Power opportunities. Importantly, during periods when contributing money is not optimal, you can still be working your plan: studying the best charities, weighing your best giving options, donating your time or services, and earning the money today you will give later. The existence of a lifetime giving plan can act like a North Star in your life.

This life-cycle perspective on charitable giving is underscored by three dynamics that broadly vector in the same direction.

1. **Your wisdom about giving to charity is likely to increase over time.**

Giving choices made later in life will probably be more robust than giving choices made when you are young. While a life cycle perspective still applies even if your charitable giving choices do not improve, if you become a more astute giver, this can add tremendous value.

It makes sense to postpone spending while knowledge is being acquired. The smarter giving you could have done tomorrow is wasted by premature donations today.

In most cases, this learning will come from reading significant books and journal articles in your area of philanthropic interest. Treat this like an academic course. Follow the leading experts in your area on X (previously known as Twitter) or LinkedIn. Learn about the major agencies doing work in the field. No matter how much money you have, it will be easy to misallocate it unless you become a shrewd charity shopper.

Charities are used to dealing with donors who are more passive and less knowledgeable than you will be. Their fundraising is targeted at people who support their work but who, due to other commitments, have limited bandwidth for their message. You, on the other hand, will be a whip-smart, dangerous (because so well-informed) giver. While your giving timetable may not correspond with the annual fundraising campaigns, charities will be happy to engage with you, and their patience will be rewarded.

### 2. Your wealth will compound over time.

Invested properly, it should compound faster than the good it would do if spent now. The one dollar given to charity today does not remain in the stock market to become two inflation-adjusted dollars in eleven years. The invisible dollars that have disappeared from your account are the hidden cost of the dollar given today.

Conventional life cycle investing suggests that people start their investing careers 100% invested in stocks and then gradually add bonds or cash to lower their risk profile as retirement nears (i.e., as their human capital diminishes and their labor income is replaced by financial capital from saving and investing—on the way to becoming social capital in the form of charitable donations). Figure 12.1 shows the hypothetical inflation-adjusted growth of one dollar over the life cycle. This dollar is invested 100% in U.S. stocks at age 21; then the portfolio switches to 60% stocks/40% bonds at age 36 and switches again to 50% stocks/50% bonds at age 56 and stays there for the duration. Many variations can work; this is simply one example.

Figure 12.1: Growth of $1

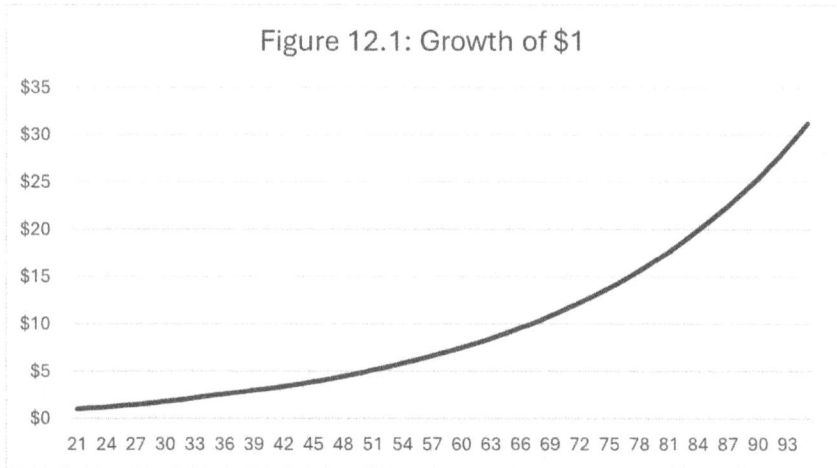

You can see the opportunity cost of giving today by comparing any two points along the curve. For example, the $1 you give away at age 21 in the chart would buy $10 worth of charity at age 68. These are the trade-offs.

One fortunate consequence is that the best investment approach for charitable dollars largely coincides with a recommended life-cycle investment approach for young people, that is, an all-equity (or even a levered equity) investment. Because young people have so few dollars in savings, it is important to maximize their growth. This way, their dollars will have a chance to grow into a lot of money later and pay for their retirements. Investing too conservatively in your twenties and thirties can be a serious mistake. People see a menu of funds in their 401(k) plans and pick a half-dozen, watering down their returns. Even if they lose money on an all-stock portfolio during a market dip, the risk is still low because these dollar amounts are minuscule relative to the value of their human capital. They have the luxury of time for their stock investments to recover.

Taken in isolation, one might conclude that the best strategy for charitable giving would be to save money all your life and leave it to charity in your estate. Or, even better, leave it in a charitable trust from your estate to compound for another century. In 1789, Ben Franklin left half his estate to accumulate for two hundred years and then donated it to the State of Pennsylvania. But this is not usually the best course.

You don't want to be like one of these people we occasionally read about in the newspaper who save every penny, live on Ritz crackers in some dingy apartment, and then die leaving millions of dollars to Shamu the whale. Your engagement is part of the equation. We are counting on your growing sophistication to oversee directing these dollars to useful pursuits. Your giving wisdom should tell you there is a high probability that money spent long after you are gone will be appropriated or wasted on the way.

3. **The tax code will punish giving when you are young and poor but amplify your charitable investment later in life when you are richer.**

Other things equal, you should prefer to donate the most dollars to charity during years when your Giving Power is highest. This insight is sufficiently powerful that you will do far more good if you make it the centerpiece of your charitable planning instead of an afterthought.

Hence, this book. A flat tax across all types of income with no tax deductions would negate this tax advantage. However, a tax code that simple and transparent would offer no fundraising opportunities to politicians. We will never see it.

Broadly, we think that you will be getting smarter about charitable giving over time, that you will save and invest money appropriately for your age, and that you will be taxed at higher rates as your income rises over the decades. Most people will receive no tax break from giving through their estates, which promotes the idea of giving during high-earning years once the hurdle of saving for retirement has been cleared.

## Your Twenties through Your Forties

The idea is to use this time to exploit your human capital, which you can leverage over the coming decades to create financial capital, with any surplus becoming available as social capital for charitable giving.

It usually will be better for you not to give to charity at this point except in token amounts. Your circumstances likely offer you no tax-fueled "Giving Power," but more likely a tax "Giving Penalty" equal to the negative of your marginal income tax rate. This is because you are not able to get any benefit for itemizing charitable deductions. You are giving when it will be at its most expensive ("least bang for the buck") at exactly the time when you have the fewest discretionary dollars to spend and numerous important competing uses for your next dollar. The notable exception would be if your employer offers a giving match, presenting you with an opportunity for leveraged giving, at least for the limited sums it might be prudent for you to donate at this point.

It is naïve to give away a lot of money as a young adult because there is a wide range of possible outcomes over your lifetime.

Post-World War II life in the United States has been a story of sustained and triumphant material progress, but this is unusual in world historical experience. As young adults, the urgent task of planning for your future is before you. Now is the time to finish your education, fund a Roth IRA, Health Savings Account, 529 plan (if you have children), start a 401(k)/403(b)/457 plan at work, open a brokerage investment account, and buy a home. Secure your own oxygen mask first, then worry about helping your neighbor. Otherwise, you risk eventually becoming an object of charity yourself.

Before making donations as a young adult or in middle age, check whether you can afford to by using a tool like ETFMathGuy's free *Pre-Retirement Savings Forecasting Tool* to make sure your savings are on track:

https://apps.etfmathguy.com/savings

The exception would be if you are a wealthy young playboy like Bruce Wayne. Otherwise, your main donation should take the form of using your valuable time to research charitable causes of interest and importance. I suggest that you conceptualize this broadly. As Calvin Coolidge said, "The man who builds a factory builds a temple." Your labor not only funds the specific charitable giving you might do later, but also powers capitalism's useful course in lifting humanity out of poverty (with the peripheral benefits of nutrition, education, health care, and general well-being flowing outward in a virtuous circle.) For most people, the fruits of their productive labor will probably do more good for more people than their charitable giving will.

Young people are often passionate about causes but lack a broader knowledge of how the world works and the best ways to achieve the ends they seek. They underappreciate self-interested "agency" problems and overrate the likelihood of big wins from government programs. Young people may link themselves to a cause as part of their transition to an adult identity. They may be prey to peer pressure, groupthink, and pied pipers who want to exploit them. We are all impatient for a better world, but achieving one is obviously not easy or we would already be living in it. You will still be here tomorrow, but your current dreams may not.

With the arrow of time, people grow up. They acquire more seasoned, enduring, and better-thought-through ideas on how charity dollars might be directed.

You may object that the need is now. Certainly, charity administrators would like your money today. They have their own goals to accomplish on their own timetables, and payrolls to meet. Their successors will worry about the problems of the future. But your charity—assuming they remain number one on your Hit Parade—will be well paid to wait. You might be able to give twice as much a decade from now. Is the donation today so urgent that it is worth double the donation you might give later? Perhaps in particular cases, but on average, probably not. As is well-known in charity circles, most urgent humanitarian crises are almost impossible to address with charitable donations at the time. Yet this is when charitable appeals crop up, because charities know this is when the public feels the greatest need to give. Every crisis is a fundraising opportunity. During one international crisis, I heard about a famous charity that helicoptered in a film crew to capture them for fundraising footage, even though they contributed nothing to its amelioration.

One other point about waiting. We live in an unusual time—the world has grown richer and teems with billionaire philanthropists. Warren Buffett. Bill Gates. Melinda Gates. Dustin Moskovitz. The Koch brothers. Jeremy Grantham. Jeff Bezos. MacKenzie Scott. Michael Soros. Mark Zuckerberg. Priscilla Chan. Charles Feeney. Azim Premji. Eli and Edyth Broad. Larry Ellison. Sergey Brin. David Rubenstein. Ted Turner. Paul Allen. Michael Bloomberg. Elon Musk. Bill Ackman. Seth Klarman. Richard Branson. In fact, 240 billionaires (and counting) have now signed the Giving Pledge, promising to donate some $600 billion to charity. Are you better at spotting giving opportunities than these philanthropists, a number of whom have been devoting their lives to philanthropy, bringing immense practical experience, fantastic connections, and major real-world accomplishments to the table along with their money? I do not see much downside in letting the billionaires have a run at their best ideas. We can always pile on later.

## Your Fifties and Sixties

By midlife, you are likely reaching your peak earning years. You will have a sense of your financial trajectory. You can probably size up whether your parents will need financial support. You will know what it will take to see your children through school. You might be aware of special needs that you couldn't have foreseen in your twenties. In other words, you are able to construct a realistic financial plan. This plan will reveal whether you can afford to do charitable giving today. Absent such a plan, or absent sizable wealth, you probably should not be giving away significant sums. Armed with a plan, you can right-size your charitable donations while trying to do the most good per dollar, making you an effective giver.

A rule of thumb: if you are not itemizing (or close to itemizing) deductions on Schedule A and instead taking the standard deduction, you will not get the best deal from Uncle Sam for your charitable donations. Your best bet will probably be to donate some highly appreciated stock from your brokerage account to a donor-advised fund, which would let you spread the distributions to your charities over the years ahead.

This is a time to devise your best strategy for the back nine. Look at your retirement date, the likely RMDs from your retirement accounts, Social Security, pensions, annuities, interest and dividends from your investment portfolio—the works. Then add in all the above for your spouse. Consider your likely future tax rates. Think about the tax brackets for your heirs, and consider whether it might be more advantageous for you to do Roth conversions of your Traditional IRAs now or let your heirs pay the taxes when they inherit them (but of course not if your IRA beneficiary is a charity that pays no taxes).

These are complicated problems, and it takes financial planning software to crack them. If you have a financial advisor, you probably have access to one of these programs. I hope that the major software packages will expand their efforts to facilitate charitable planning along the lines we have sketched. In the meantime, ETFMathGuy's online retirement income calculator is excellent:

https://apps.etfmathguy.com/calc

If the free version's analysis indicates that Roth conversions add economic value to your retirement or estate plan, upgrade to the paid version so you can fold these costs and benefits into your lifetime giving plan.

Regarding charitable giving, does the analysis show that you are on track to retire with a comfortable margin of safety so that you won't outlive your savings? If not, giving money to charity for the present is a luxury you cannot afford.

If you can afford to give, how much? Plug different numbers into your annual aftertax spending and see what works. Check the answers by changing parameters like longevity, tax rates, inflation rates, and investment returns and rerun the numbers until you have a robust answer. This is not a one-and-done exercise. Repeat it every year before you donate to make sure your retirement is on track.

If your financial cushion is low or borderline, skip charitable giving for now and work it into your estate plan instead. The easiest way would be to make a charity the backup beneficiary on your IRA.

If you are a motivated giver and your cushion is adequate, consider a combo plan like Renee #1 used in the last chapter:

- Give appreciated stock to a donor-advised fund the final year you are employed full-time

- Salt away enough money in the DAF to cover your annual giving until you start taking required minimum distributions from your IRA at age 73 or 75
- Switch to taking Qualified Charitable Distributions from your IRA

Weigh the giving power of appreciated stock vs. qualified charitable distributions from your IRA in case one approach works markedly better than the other. The QCDs have no hurdle to cross from the standard deduction, and so do not require a large upfront commitment or annual maintenance expense. If you are unsure, wait until you start taking the required minimum distributions from your IRA to examine whether qualified charitable distributions are an affordable option.

## But what about Tithing?

Tithing will typically provide larger contributions over your career as you advance in income and tax brackets. But the overall analysis presented in this book points to a different solution than giving a flat 10% of your income away every year.

If God wants you to tithe, then you should tithe. There are a surprising number of tithing permutations, and I recommend

Dr. Jim Dahle's (*The White Coat Investor*) excellent online article, "How Much Should I Tithe to My Church?"

## To Infinity and Beyond

Are you charitably inclined, with enough money to have an estate tax problem? This raises the question of whether it would have been smarter to give away more money earlier in life so that you stayed under the estate tax threshold. It is easier to toss an acorn over a fence than to relocate an oak tree. In that sense, the Giving Power of any charitable donation earlier would be amplified by a reduction in your estate tax later. Absent clairvoyance, this is difficult to plan unless you anticipate having an estate greater than whatever estate tax exemption will be in force at the time of your departure. If the exemption turns out to be low, many gifts you made earlier would lead to estate tax exclusions later.

Congress refuses to give us a simple tax code. Since they change it frequently to placate their various benefactors, tax planning is unnecessarily difficult. In 2001, the estate tax exemption was $675,000. In 2002, it was $1 million. By 2009, it had risen to $3.5 million. Then, in 2010, there was no estate tax. By 2017, it was over $5 million, and in 2025, the exemption will be $13.99 million, but slated to go down to perhaps $7.2 million in 2026 unless the Republicans reinstate it first. The point is, you may not be able to do reliable estate tax planning until late in life.

For the richest among us, the adjusted gross income limitations on charitable giving during our lifetimes impede giving sooner to charity. Billionaires can afford to arrange their financial lives so that their taxable income is as small as possible. Millionaires typically do not have this luxury, and so are taxed at higher rates than billionaires. Due to his low salary and considering the AGI limits, the first $41 billion Warren Buffett donated to charity only had a Giving Power of 0.04%. He did, however, remove the money and its future growth from his estate, so it was really more like 40.04% if that is any consolation. Almost all of his estate is going to charity anyway. Deciding when to decumulate a large fortune for philanthropic purposes is a complicated decision. The Adjusted Gross Income limits discourage predeath giving for the richest among us, and so postpone for decades the social good this money might otherwise do.

People are better advised to give to charity during their lifetimes rather than through their estates. As Sears founder and philanthropist Julius Rosenwald succinctly put it, "Give while you live." The worst case would be to use your will to start a perpetual foundation since after twenty years that foundation is unlikely to be recognizably aligned with your values and intentions. Another way of putting this: while the ability to compound money continues after your death, whatever posthumous instructions you leave will be ignored sooner or later, probably sooner. The family might show some deference to your wishes for a time, but professional administrators can be counted on to run the show for their own benefit.

Life-cycle charitable planning is what many great philanthropists have done. Philanthropists made fortunes during their working life and then gave their money away. A recent example is Warren Buffett. The original plan was for Warren to make money (what he did best) and for his wife Susie to give it to charity (what she did best). But then Susie died, while Warren kept making money. When his friends Bill and Melinda Gates started their Foundation, this became the giving vehicle he was looking for – one large enough to absorb his billions without being swamped by them. More recently, he decided to channel the remainder of his charity dollars through his three children. All the funds will be disbursed to charity within ten years of his passing.

In this book, I have tried scaling down what big philanthropists have done to fit the rest of us. Even if you have no interest in developing a lifetime giving plan, you can still use it to figure out your best options for giving today.

\* \* \*

Gentle reader, I hope you have gotten a useful idea or two out of this book. I wasn't kidding when I said to run them past your legal, tax, and financial advisors. As I learn about any errors that have crept in, I will call them out on my website, www.phildemuth.com.

# Glossary

*501(c)(3) organizations*: Tax-exempt charitable organizations, including religious, educational, and scientific entities, with tax-deductible contributions for donors.

*501(c)(4) organizations*: Tax-exempt social welfare organizations that may engage in some political activities, but donor contributions are generally not tax-deductible.

*7520 Rate*: An interest rate published monthly by the IRS, used to value certain charitable gifts and calculate split-interest trust payouts, among other things.

*"Above the line" deduction*: Deductions taken before calculating your Adjusted Gross Income (AGI) on page 1, line 11, of Form 1040, directly reducing overall taxable income.

*"Below the line" deduction*: Deductions taken after calculating AGI, typically itemized on Schedule A of Form 1040. These are less efficient than "above the line" deductions.

*"Bunching" tax deductions*: Concentrating deductible expenses into a single tax year to exceed the standard deduction threshold in order to maximize the tax savings from charitable donations.

*Adjusted Gross Income (AGI)*: Total gross income minus certain specific deductions, used to calculate taxable income and determine eligibility for certain tax benefits.

*AGI Limitations*: Restrictions on the amount of charitable contributions that can be deducted, based on a percentage of the donor's AGI.

*Average Tax Rate:* the total amount of taxes paid divided by the total taxable income.

*Capital Gains*: Profit from selling capital assets, such as stocks or property, and taxed at different rates depending on the holding period and income level.

*Carry-forward provisions*: Rules allowing unused deductions or credits to be applied to future tax years.

*Charitable Gift Annuity*: A contract where a donor gives assets to a charity in exchange for a fixed income stream for life, with the remainder benefiting the charity.

*CLAT (Charitable Lead Annuity Trust)*: A trust that provides fixed payments to a charity for a set term, with remaining assets typically passing to family beneficiaries.

*CRUT (Charitable Remainder Unitrust)*: A trust paying a fixed percentage of its assets to beneficiaries annually, with the remainder going to charity upon termination.

*Direct Indexing*: An investment strategy replicating an index by directly owning each of its component stocks individually.

*Donor-Advised Funds*: Charitable giving accounts allowing donors to contribute assets, receive an immediate tax deduction, and recommend grants from their account over time.

*Employer Matching Gift*: A program where employers match employees' charitable donations, often at a 1:1 ratio up to some specified limit.

*ESG Investing*: An investment strategy considering environmental, social, and governance factors alongside financial metrics.

*Estate Tax*: Tax on the transfer of property at death, applying to estates exceeding a certain threshold, and currently set at 40% at the federal level

*Fair Market Value*: The price an asset would sell for on the open market between a willing buyer and seller.

*Giving Power*: A measure of the tax efficiency of charitable giving, calculated by dividing the tax saving (or tax penalty) dollars by the total amount donated to charity

*Index Fund*: A mutual fund or exchange-traded fund designed to track the performance of a specific market index such as the S&P 500, and often featuring a lower expense ratio and better performance than similar actively managed funds.

*Life-Cycle Planning*: A financial planning approach that considers different life stages and changing financial needs over time.

*Marginal Tax Rate:* the tax rate applied to the last dollar of taxable income earned

*Pooled Income Fund*: A type of charitable trust where multiple donors' gifts are combined for investment purposes, with income paid to beneficiaries and remainder to charity.

*Private Foundation*: A nongovernmental, nonprofit organization with funds managed by its own trustees or directors, typically funded by a single source.

*Private Operating Foundation*: A type of private foundation that directly engages in charitable activities rather than primarily making grants.

*Prudent Investor Rule*: A legal standard requiring fiduciaries to invest trust assets as a prudent investor would, considering the entire portfolio.

*Qualified Charitable Distributions (QCDs)*: Direct transfers from IRAs to qualified charities, allowing individuals over $70\frac{1}{2}$ to donate up to $108,000 annually without counting toward taxable income.

*Required Minimum Distributions (RMDs)*: Minimum amounts that retirement plan account owners must withdraw annually, now starting at age 73.

*SECURE Act*: Legislation passed in 2019 affecting retirement savings rules, including changes to RMD age and inherited IRA distributions.

*Standard Deduction*: A fixed dollar amount that reduces taxable income, set by the IRS annually, which taxpayers can claim instead of itemizing deductions. It simplifies tax filing and is used by most taxpayers who don't have significant deductible expenses.

*Supporting Organizations*: Public charities that support other tax-exempt organizations, usually through fundraising and grant-making.

*Tax Credit*: A dollar-for-dollar reduction in tax liability, more valuable than a deduction of the same amount.

*Tax Deduction*: An expense subtracted from income before calculating taxes owed, reducing taxable income.

*Tax Cuts and Jobs Act*: Major tax reform legislation passed under the Trump administration in 2017, significantly lowering individual and corporate tax rates.

*Testamentary Gift Annuity*: A charitable gift annuity funded through a will or trust, taking effect after the donor's death.

*Tithing*: Practice of giving a tenth of one's income, typically to a religious organization or charity.

# Acknowledgments

I thank the following members of the Legion of Super-Heroes for their invaluable advice along the way:

- Geoff Considine
- Jim DiLellio
- Alan Gassman
- James Picerno

Let's not forget to thank the following influencers:

- Randy Abeles
- Ted Batson
- Stephen Bigge
- Natalie Choate
- Paige Goepfert
- Laura Hinson
- Christopher Hoyt
- Holly Isdale
- Bob Keebler
- Michael Kitces

- Jeff Levine
- Justin Miller
- Ed Slott
- Rick Springer
- Jimmy Williams

Conversations or readings from many people have influenced my thinking about charitable giving. Some of these include:

- The Bogleheads
- Warren Buffett
- Paul Brest
- Tyler Cowen
- Shelby Davis
- Christopher DeMuth
- Nicolas Duquette
- Gordon Irlam
- Peter D. Kaufman
- Holden Karnofsky
- Charlie Munger
- Bruce Steiner

While I have tried to learn from all these people, this is not to imply that any of them would agree with my lucubrations. This little book was written over several years, and undoubtedly there are others whose intellectual property I have inadvertently appropriated without acknowledgment. Sorry!

# About the Author

*Phil at the Whisky a Go Go*

Phil DeMuth was valedictorian at the University of California at Santa Barbara, and then went on for his Ph.D. in clinical psychology. This is his tenth book on wealth management.

By day, Phil runs Conservative Wealth Management LLC in Los Angeles, but at night his mission is to bring wholesome rock and roll music to the scenesters of the Sunset Strip.

www.phildemuth.com

www.ingramcontent.com/pod-product-compliance
Lightning Source LLC
Chambersburg PA
CBHW031403180326
41458CB00043B/6596/J